W9-BNY-930

TREASURES OF ASIA

COLLECTION PLANNED BY

ALBERT SKIRA

TREASURES OF ASIA

CHINESE PAINTING

TEXT BY JAMES CAHILL

Former Associate Curator of Chinese Art at the Freer Gallery of Art, Washington, D.C.

SKIRA

RIZZOLI
NEW YORK

Color plate on the title page:
Tao-chi (1641-c. 1717): The Waterfall on Mount Lu. Detail from a hanging scroll.
Ink and light colors on silk. Collection of the late Kanichi Sumitomo, Oise (Japan).

*

© 1977 by Editions d'Art Albert Skira S.A., Geneva
First edition © 1960 by Editions d'Art Albert Skira, Geneva

This edition published in the United States of America in 1985 by

*R*IZZOLI *INTERNATIONAL PUBLICATIONS, INC.*
712 Fifth Avenue/New York 10019

All rights reserved
No parts of this book may be reproduced in any manner whatsoever without permission of
Rizzoli International Publications, Inc.

Library of Congress Catalog Card Number: 76-62896
ISBN: 0-8478-0079-2

PRINTED IN SWITZERLAND

THE problem of why the Chinese tradition of painting, the richest and most diversified in world art outside Europe, has not received the attention it merits in the Occident, is treated briefly but perceptively by André Malraux in his *Museum Without Walls*. Some of the reasons he advances are material ones: good color reproductions have not been available in large enough numbers; major collections in the Far East have until recently been all but inaccessible, while those in the West (one might add, particularly in Europe) are not yet sufficient to serve as the basis for any broad acquaintance with the art. Another reason is historical: a *"fin-de-siècle* 'Japanism' ... still travesties it for us." Malraux's most provocative suggestion is that while Sung painting (no other period but Sung has found a place in his Imaginary Museum) "is beginning to whet the curiosity of our painters," its "seeming humanism answers none of our contemporary problems."

The material obstacles are fast being overcome; the present book is one contribution toward that end. The "Japanism" is fading, as we become aware of how profoundly our view of Chinese painting was affected by Japanese ideas and attitudes during the pioneering stage of our studies, and set about to replace these with the more highly developed and pertinent ideas of the Chinese, as well as with some of our own. About the "seeming humanism" there is nothing to be done. It is more than seeming, it is real. One sometimes finds it denied: as a widespread loss of faith in the Western humanistic heritage provokes a search for alternatives in remote periods and places, China is sometimes forced into an uncomfortable alliance with India and other "traditional" cultures governed by ritual and religion, in order that it might seem to offer one such alternative. But it is in fact just because the civilization of China has been, like our own in recent centuries, a humanistic civilization repeatedly beset by doubts about the validity of the humanist ideal, that its art is so completely relevant to the situation of the twentieth century West. The emergence of an aesthetic theory according to which painting serves to express the thought and feeling of the individual man, besides—or even instead of— making any descriptive, interpretative or metaphysical statement about the world around him, was a relatively early development in China, and one that could have occurred only in a humanistic context. Once this view had become the dominant one, accepted by painters as well as critics, the Chinese artist was even further removed than before from the anonymous artisan of the "traditional" society, who, the theory goes, suppressed his own personality to embody in his works concepts common to the whole culture. Matters that were not supposed to concern this selfless craftsman at all were of profound concern to the Chinese painter: how to build a style into a personal instrument of expression, how to reach a balance between objective description and subjective comment, how to endow the formal materials of the painting with a humane content, so that its meaning need not be bound to the literal or symbolic meaning of its subject matter. Although in a superficial sense the human being was not the dominant theme in Chinese painting of the Sung and later periods, in a deeper sense he was; he may not appear conspicuously in the picture, but he makes his presence felt, often obtrusively, in the style. The values attributed to painting in China, moreover, were human values. The stabilizing effect of tradition was respected, but so was individual creativity. The history of painting was seen to proceed by impulses, as major masters originated styles, giving rise sometimes to separate schools and movements. The critics recognized that each artist must begin by adopting a large part of his style from his predecessors, and tried to trace the sources of his style, but recognized also the element of free choice in it. They did not confine their attention to the art object itself, but focused it also on the painter as a man, and on the painting as a revelation of the man.

There is nothing so very exotic about all this; it seems, on the contrary, perfectly familiar. The situation has curiously reversed itself: where Chinese painting once was insufficiently understood because of its supposed strangeness, it is now in danger of being misunderstood and distorted by those who feel it is not, in its true character, strange enough. The temptation is to see it as mysterious and therefore exciting; insofar as it appears to repeat our own discoveries, we find it that much less interesting. But it has no need for spurious glamour. While many of the artistic problems dealt with by the Chinese painters were essentially the same ones that have occupied Occidental artists, modes of representation and expression were often very different, so that the Chinese solutions strike us, nearly always, as fresh and stimulating. We can decide better whether or not they "answer any of our contemporary problems" when we have come to a better understanding of them, especially as they are exemplified in particular paintings. The text that follows presents the paintings against a background of the aesthetic and critical ideas current in their respective periods and schools, and so is intended as an aid to such understanding.

We are grateful to all the museums and private collectors who gave permission for paintings they own to be photographed in color and reproduced in this book. In particular, the Joint Administration of National Palace and Central Museums in Taiwan deserves our thanks for granting us the unprecedented privilege of making fifty color transparencies of paintings in that incomparable collection, from which nearly half our plates have been made; all but a few of them are reproduced in color for the first time, and many were unpublished until now. In Japan, we are grateful to the Commission for the Protection of Cultural Properties, Tokyo, and in particular to Prof. Takaaki Matsushita, for the paintings owned by the Commission; to the Kyoto National Museum and Prof. Shūjirō Shimada, for paintings kept there; to the Osaka Municipal Museum, for paintings in the former Abe Collection; and to the Yamato Bunka-kan, Osaka; the Fujii Yūrinkan, Kyoto; and the Nezu Art Museum, Tokyo. Four Buddhist temples in Kyoto allowed us to photograph their treasured paintings: the Daitokuji, the Tōfukuji, the Ninnaji and the Shōkokuji. Among private collectors, we are grateful to Mrs. Kanichi Sumitomo, Oiso, for permission to photograph paintings in the superb collection brought together by her late husband, and to Mr. Hisao Sugahara, Kamakura.

Museums in the United States and Europe which kindly permitted us to include Chinese paintings in their possession are the Freer Gallery of Art, Washington, D.C.; the Museum of Fine Arts, Boston; The William Rockhill Nelson Gallery of Art, Kansas City; the Metropolitan Museum of Art, New York; the Honolulu Academy of Arts; the British Museum, London; and the Museum of Asiatic Art, Amsterdam. Private collectors whose paintings appear in our plates include Mr. John M. Crawford, Jr., New York; Mr. C. C. Wang, New York; Mr. H. C. Weng, Scarsdale, New York; the Nü Wa Chai Collection, Munich; and Mr. Jean-Pierre Dubosc, Lugano. I am grateful to Mr. C. C. Wang also for giving me the benefit of his connoisseurship by checking the selection of paintings and making useful suggestions concerning the authenticity and quality of certain pieces.

Prof. Max Loehr was kind enough to read through the entire manuscript critically, and a great many corrections and other changes, both minor and major, were based on his careful annotations. The text was read also by my wife, whose suggestions led to the rewriting of some passages and numerous other improvements. The translations from Chinese sources are mostly my own, but I have consulted, in connection with some of them, the seven volume *Chinese Painting* by Dr. Osvald Sirén, which served also as a reference for information about some artists. My indebtedness to his monumental work is thus greater than its mere inclusion in the Bibliography might suggest. The rendering of lines from a poem by Shen Chou on p. 127 is by Dr. Richard Edwards and Mr. Tseng Hsien-ch'i.

My text is dedicated to Mr. A. G. Wenley, the distinguished director of the Freer Gallery of Art, with warm gratitude for all his teaching.

JAMES CAHILL.

Contents

Anonymous, eighth century (?), from Tun-huang: The Paradise of Amitābha Buddha.
Hanging scroll. Ink and colors on silk. (54×40″) British Museum, London.

Early Figure Painting
The Han, Six Dynasties and T'ang Periods

1

"To paint is to draw boundaries," writes the author of the *Shuo wen*, the first Chinese dictionary, around the year A.D. 100. He explains the character for *hua*, "to paint," as representing a hand grasping a marker and drawing the four boundaries of a field, that is to say, *delineating* a field. Sixteen centuries later, the great individualist painter Tao-chi was to open his theoretical treatise by speaking of the Single Brushstroke as "the origin of all existence, the root of the myriad phenomena"—one might almost, without violating the sense, translate: "In the beginning was the Brushstroke."

In the beginning and also in the end; the line drawn by a brush remains the central fact of Chinese painting throughout its history. Painting began in Europe also as an art of line, but lost its linear character as painters turned their attention from the outlines to what they enclosed, concentrating on the rendition of light and shadow, mass and texture, softening or obscuring contours and so lessening the importance of line. The course of Chinese painting led in a different direction; its artists, never so concerned with reproducing faithfully the color and texture of surfaces or the corporeality of mass, gave ever greater emphasis to the brushline itself, taking it as their primary descriptive and expressive means. Stylistic movements that tended to destroy the integrity of the individual brushstroke, or to subordinate linear drawing to surface treatment, were generally regarded as unorthodox departures from the main tradition.

The earliest surviving examples of true painting in China are on two fragments of silk, dating from around the third century B.C., which were excavated from tombs at Ch'ang-sha in present-day Hunan Province. The pictures, drawn in fine, black ink brushline, with flat washes of color filling the areas thus bounded, exemplify already the technique, and even something of the style, that was to remain basic and orthodox for many centuries. They are symbolic representations of humans, demons, animals and plants, set off as separate images by their outlines from the neutral silk ground. This ancient mode of representation corresponds to an even more ancient mode of thought, in which "images" *(hsiang)* played an important role as abstractions of natural phenomena, objects and aspects of the world isolated from context and conceptualized. The characters of the written language in their earliest form as "pictograms" were images of one kind; another was exemplified by the hexagrams of the ancient divination text known as the *Book of Changes*, thought to be derived from the visual patterns of the physical universe. The forms created by the painter were still another. When composed into a scene, they were juxtaposed without being integrated. Between and around them was void; space had no existence except as that which separated one image from another.

The figures painted on a clay slab from a tomb of the latter part of the Han dynasty (206 B.C.-221 A.D.), now in the Museum of Fine Arts, Boston, still stand isolated against an amorphous ground. But already the artist has discovered two means of unifying his picture: through suggested movement, the figures seeming to be swayed by a common cadence, and through the mutual awareness revealed in the exchange of glances that binds them. Even a minor drawing such as this—it certainly does not represent the highest achievements of Han painting—already begins to transcend the limitations of a truly conceptual art. It shows the results of observation, although the artist almost certainly did not paint from life (Chinese painters very seldom did). The men in it are self-sufficient, conscious individuals, not merely symbols or stereotypes. They are not, moreover, minor players in a cosmic drama, for whatever the subject of the painting may be (it has not been clearly identified) it is apparently not in any way religious. The greatest Han painting, as reported in the literature of that period, was secular. Confucianism, representing the rationalistic and human-centered side of Chinese thought, had become dominant in state and society, and its influence extended to painting: pictures of edifying subjects, the Confucianists maintained, performed a moral function in society, refining the spirit and elevating the minds of men. Portraits of eminent personages of the past, illustrations to historical anecdotes or classical texts, were most esteemed.

The lineament in which the figures on the Boston tile are drawn, while it has not yet realized the full potentialities of the Chinese brush—perhaps the most versatile and responsive drawing implement devised by man—suggests that painters may have been experimenting already with idiomatic brushwork. Fluctuations in breadth of line serve to enliven the drawing with an air of spontaneity, to accent contours, to intensify that sense of movement which seems to have been the objective of much of Han art. One of the chief criteria of excellence in Chinese painting throughout its history is quality of brushline. The same brush was used for writing, and the brilliant rise of the art of calligraphy in the Han and later dynasties was eventually to affect profoundly the technique of painting. But not until much later; the relaxed brushwork of the Boston tile persists only in similarly informal sketches, while the thin, even line of the most ancient style, with little of calligraphic character, remains standard for centuries in more finished works.

The disintegration of the Han empire in the early third century A.D. was followed by a long period of division into smaller states, none of which succeeded in conquering the others and ruling the whole territory of China until the end of the sixth century. We know the names of many artists who were active during the intervening Six Dynasties period, and a little about what their contemporaries thought of them, for this is the age that produced the first critical literature on painting. The only artist of the period whose

Anonymous (second or third century A.D.): Figures painted on a tomb tile.
Ink and colors on a clay surface. (H. 7⅝″) Museum of Fine Arts, Boston.

此之由

Attributed to Ku K'ai-chih (born c. 345): Admonitions to the Court Ladies. Section of a handscroll.
Ink and colors on silk. (H. 9¾″) British Museum, London.

name is attached to any surviving pictures of real antiquity, however, is Ku K'ai-chih, born around the year 345. He was famous not only for his painting, but also for his eccentric speech and behavior. His contemporaries credited him with "pre-eminence in three fields: wit, painting and foolishness."

Nothing so very eccentric can be detected in the paintings attributed to him; only a touch of playfulness, at most. The earliest and finest among them, the handscroll in the British Museum titled *Admonitions to the Court Ladies*, belongs to that didactic kind of painting favored by the early Confucianists, illustrating a fourth century moralizing text which is made up of advice on matters of deportment delivered to ladies of the imperial harem by the Court Preceptress. The passage of text that precedes the ninth picture in the scroll contains the words: "No one can endlessly please; affection cannot be for one alone; if it be so, it will one day end in disgust." A graceful court lady appears to be learning this bitter truth as the emperor repulses her with a gesture. The long bands of cloth fluttering from her clothing, as if blown by the wind or agitated by rapid movement, are later echoes of the swift linear plays used in Han dynasty drawing to impart a sense of vitality to the picture. As painters grew more proficient in the descriptive rendering of action, the need for such artifices disappeared; an entire mass might be convincingly portrayed in motion.

The painting is in the form of a handscroll, or horizontal scroll, which is designed to be unrolled section by section, in such a way that no more than two feet or so is seen at a time. The materials and technique are the usual ones for the early period: fine drawing in ink line, and washes of water color, on silk. In orthodox Chinese styles the color washes are flat and ungraduated; color is almost never used as it is in the West, to model form or to describe the fall of light on a surface. The use of shading in some portions of the *Admonitions* scroll is one feature of several that point to a later date for the painting, some centuries after the time of Ku K'ai-chih. But in its composition and drawing, it is probably based closely on a work by Ku or some other Six Dynasties master.

The technique of illusionistic shading, to give plasticity to the forms of painting, was introduced to China from the West, along with the doctrine and iconography of Buddhism. One of the first masters to put it to effective use was Chang Seng-yu, an early sixth century artist whose major output consisted of wall paintings for Buddhist temples. The Chinese were quite unfamiliar with this device, which was remotely derived from the late classical art of the Mediterranean region and transmitted to China by way of northern India and the oasis cities of Central Asia. Chang's paintings must have been startling and a bit disturbing in their time; old conventions were being violated. But the Chinese tended to be tolerant of innovations and experiments, not nearly so artistically reactionary as the Occidental myths have them. The practice of shading, although it seems never to have progressed much beyond a simple stage, was carried on into the T'ang dynasty, and appears occasionally even later.

Another innovation of Chang Seng-yu, probably also of western derivation, was a more fleshy figure type. A ninth century writer characterizes the great early figure painters by saying that Ku K'ai-chih captured the souls of his subjects, Lu T'an-wei (a fifth century master) their bones, and Chang Seng-yu their flesh. A well-known handscroll attributed to Chang, the *Five Planets and Twenty-eight Constellations*, exhibits both the technique of shading and an increased corporeality in the figures. It is quite possibly based on designs of Chang Seng-yu, although the copy may be as late as the eleventh or twelfth century. It is made up, like the *Admonitions* scroll attributed to Ku K'ai-chih, of a series of pictures, separated by passages of text—in this case, descriptions of the deities and instructions on how they should be worshipped. The figures are set against blank areas of silk, again as in the *Admonitions*. But the two pictures, even as copies, reveal a change in attitude; in the *Planets* scroll, a new sobriety has supplanted the playfulness of Ku K'ai-chih. The lineament is tamer; the naïveté of the earliest styles has already been lost.

The Chen-hsing, the planet Saturn, is portrayed as an emaciated old man seated cross-legged on the back of an ox. The dark tone of the man's skin, along with his large nose, bulbous forehead and general hirsuteness, are common Chinese conventions for representing holy men of India and other western lands, and are often encountered in the Arhat pictures of later centuries. One suspects the ethnocentric Chinese of feeling that people of such outlandish appearance had no choice but to turn to a life of the spirit, being so obviously unfitted for urbane society. The accentuation of muscle and bone structure beneath the skin seems primitive if compared to the products of a Renaissance European artist's semi-scientific occupation with anatomy, but was no doubt a triumph of realism in its day.

The long period of division of the empire ended when, in 589, China was reunited under a single dynasty, the Sui. But by the end of the century, revolts had broken out again, and in 618 the Sui was overthrown by a new dynasty, the T'ang, which lasted nearly three hundred years. During the first half of this period, the peak of Chinese national power, there was prosperity in all spheres of life: military campaigns pushed the limits of Chinese domination far to the west, a flourishing foreign trade was carried on, and Buddhism, which had been imported from India as early as the Han dynasty, was stronger than ever before or after. It was during the T'ang dynasty that the greatest Chinese poetry was composed, and, in the categories of religious and secular figure compositions and portraits, the greatest pictures painted. So, at least, the Chinese critics tell us, and we can only accept their judgement, since the meager quantity of extant T'ang painting, or even of trustworthy copies of T'ang painting, hardly allows us to form any broad judgements of our own.

The achievements of the T'ang dynasty in figure painting may be observed if we place a small picture executed around the end of that period, the portrait of Fu Sheng now in the Osaka Municipal Museum, beside the painting attributed to Chang Seng-yu. A new flexibility is evident in the drawing; the formality of the archaic lineament has relaxed. There are fewer long curves, less compulsion to continue the line in unbroken sweeps, to simplify contours and reduce interior drawing. The short, deft strokes defining the withered skin of Fu Sheng's arms, the bony structure of his sunken chest, the wrinkles in his neck, the expressive lines on his cheek and brow, would have seemed arbitrary and intrusive in the pictures attributed to Ku K'ai-chih and Chang Seng-yu. A T'ang dynasty critic appears to recognize this difference in distinguishing the style of Ku K'ai-chih from that of later painters: Ku's lines, he says, "are firm and tense and connect with one another uninterruptedly; they circle back upon themselves in sudden rushes."

Fu Sheng was a Confucian scholar who took part in the early Han dynasty revival of classical learning in which scholarship attempted to repair the losses it had suffered through the infamous "Burning of the Books." He produced a copy of the *Book of Documents* which he had preserved by hiding it in the wall of his house and devoted the short remaining period of his life to transmitting his understanding of the text in a series of expository lectures. He is portrayed as delivering one of these, holding the scroll

Attributed to Chang Seng-yu, early sixth century (copy of the eleventh or twelfth century?):
The Planet Saturn, from The Five Planets and Twenty-eight Constellations. Section of a handscroll.
Ink and colors on silk. (H. 10¾″) Osaka Municipal Museum (former Abe Collection).

Anonymous, ninth century? (attributed to Wang Wei, 699-759): Portrait of the Scholar Fu Sheng.
Section of a handscroll. Ink and colors on silk. (H. 10¼") Osaka Municipal Museum (former Abe Collection).

in one hand and pointing with the other to a difficult passage. A benevolent smile expresses his contentment; the pupil grasps his meaning, and the truth will not be lost. Nowhere else in Chinese painting is the Confucian love of learning, the passion of the literatus for preserving the knowledge of the past together with his own insights, so well set forth.

The painting has been ascribed since the eleventh century to the great T'ang poet-painter Wang Wei, who is more celebrated for the development of ink-monochrome landscape than for his figure painting. While the portrait of Fu Sheng is not in monochrome, the coloring is subdued, limited to tinges of red along contours for the flesh and light washes elsewhere. Artists from the mid-T'ang period onward came to rely even less than before on color, more on the descriptive and expressive power of brushline alone. The painter proclaimed as the greatest master of the dynasty, Wu Tao-tzu (none of whose works survive, even in reliable copies), used only thin washes of color, or none at all. The more conservative court artists, however, continued to draw in fine line and to add bright mineral pigments. Two of them, Chang Hsüan and Chou Fang, specialized in pictures of palace ladies. Both worked in the eighth century, Chang in the first half and Chou in the second.

At least two works of Chang Hsüan are preserved in copies. The best known is the handscroll titled *Ladies Preparing Newly-woven Silk,* copied in the early twelfth century by the Emperor Hui-tsung. An everyday scene in the women's quarters of the palace is idealized and turned to the evocation of a quiet mood. Two women stretch a bolt of silk between them. Another irons, using a metal pan filled with burning coals. A girl holds the opposite edge of the cloth; a younger one, too small to be of any help, runs underneath. While there is still a certain static quality to the scene, some movement is convincingly suggested in the attitude of the lady ironing and in the off-balance pose of the one further left, repeated by the even more unstable figure of the child. This nice interplay of motion and rest, balanced and unbalanced masses, was quite beyond the reach of the Six Dynasties artist, who depended upon impetuous rushes of line to animate his designs.

T'ang painters, like T'ang sculptors, were occupied with the rendering of volume and movement, besides applying themselves to the special pictorial concern of group composition in space. Chang Hsüan's solution to this latter problem is simple but satisfying: the placing of the four main figures at corners of an imaginary lozenge laid on the ground plane establishes a sufficient depth in the picture, and no indication of setting is necessary. The arrangement is repeated in the main group of a second surviving copy after a Chang Hsüan design, a copy probably made about the same time as the other, i.e. in the eleventh or twelfth century. It represents Lady Kuo-kuo and two other sisters of the imperial consort Yang Kuei-fei riding forth on an outing with their attendants. The two pictures agree in many other points besides their compositions: the drawing of the costumes and the brocade designs on them, blue or green tracery over white, gold over red; the faces and coiffures of the women; the little girls—it might almost be the same child who appears in both.

The paintings attributed to Chou Fang, the later eighth century master of palace scenes, are no more likely to be T'ang originals than those connected with Chang Hsüan, but even as copies they reflect a different personality. The subjects are the same: the occupations and amusements of court ladies. In the small picture in the Freer Gallery, two of them are playing Double Sixes, a game similar to backgammon, while another

After Chang Hsüan, eighth century (twelfth century copy [?] attributed to Li Kung-lin):
Lady Kuo-kuo and Her Sisters Setting Forth on an Outing. Section of a handscroll.
Ink and colors on silk. (H. 13¼″) Palace Museum Collection, Taichung.

stands gazing down at them, leaning on the shoulder of a girl. The faces are impassive, as they tend to be in Chinese portrayals of well-bred subjects; but, unlike the faces in the scrolls after Chang Hsüan, these disclose a thoughtful bent in the minds behind them. No profound intelligence or individuality, to be sure; rather a consciousness, discernible in the sidelong glances, and even more in the postures: the tilt of a head, a poised hand. One can begin to note here a degree of psychological insight into the relationship between the players, and between these and their standing friend; or into the reverie of the girl on whom this friend leans, her gaze fixed outward almost toward the spectator and yet withdrawn (all this in a few simple lines).

To speak here of personal relationships sensitively captured is not to credit the artist with a precocious mastery of psychological portraiture. The picture tells us nothing about the participants beyond defining their roles in this particular scene. It is rather a distillation of the quality of a single moment in their lives, with no implications beyond that moment. The painting is precisely what it appears to be; it is not a pictorial allegory, nor is there any of the extraneous overlay—humor, drama, pathos, sentiment—that is so often present in Occidental genre art. Such a detached approach to an everyday subject may call to mind Vermeer or Chardin; but Chou Fang is less concerned than they with technical problems of representing light and space, more with the embodying of mood. Or perhaps, rather than a limited mood, something more profound and less specific: the very nature of sentient existence, that intensified awareness of the passing moment which is common to so much of Chinese literature and art from early times, and which is later made much of, as if it were an invention of their own, by the Ch'an (Zen) Buddhists.

So far we have been considering the secular painting of the T'ang dynasty. The largest body of paintings extant from the period, however, is Buddhist. It has been preserved in the Caves of the Thousand Buddhas near Tun-huang, in western Kansu Province, in the far northwest of China. As the westernmost Buddhist stronghold in China on the pilgrimage route that extended across Central Asia to India, Tun-huang was

After Chang Hsüan, eighth century (copy by Emperor Hui-tsung, early twelfth century):
Ladies Preparing Newly-woven Silk. Section of a handscroll. Ink and colors on silk. (H. 14½")
Museum of Fine Arts, Boston.

Attributed to Chou Fang, eighth century: Ladies Playing Double Sixes. Detail from a handscroll.
Ink and colors on silk. (H. 12½″) Freer Gallery of Art, Washington, D.C.

a point of entrance for foreign styles; it was also in close contact with the metropolitan centers of China, where the major artists were at work. The greater part of Tun-huang painting, in both quantity and quality, remains in the caves, painted on the walls. A large number of mobile paintings on silk and paper were also found there, however, marvelously preserved by the dry climate of the region.

One of the best-known is the large composition in the British Museum usually called the Paradise of Amitābha Buddha, but tentatively identified by Arthur Waley as a representation of the historical Buddha, Śākyamuni, delivering his first sermon under the Bodhi tree. The Buddha, whichever it may be, is engaged in preaching the doctrine, as is shown by the position of his hands. On either side are Bodhisattvas, beings who mediate between the Buddha and humankind, and monks, the disciples of Buddha. A seated woman, one of the donors, is in the lower left corner; the portrait of the male donor, originally in the lower right, is missing. The painting seems to belong to the later eighth century, but is probably based on a seventh century design. The original was no doubt executed with greater sensitivity; a degree of hardness and some awkward passages in the drawing (particularly of hands) warn us against supposing that it reflects very accurately the most advanced Chinese styles of its period. In certain features—the faces and poses of the Bodhisattvas, the bronze coloring of exposed flesh, and especially the white highlights on noses, cheeks, eyelids and chins—it seems to owe something to Central Asian Buddhist art. The coloring is exceptionally lovely, with the brightest hues concentrated in the costume of the Buddha, a brilliant red robe with green lining, and in the rich azurite blue of the hair. The painting, although it cannot be more than a dim reflection of the great Buddhist compositions of the T'ang dynasty, remains impressive, a majestic conception rendered with firm conviction.

Early Landscape Painting
Six Dynasties to Early Sung

2

THROUGHOUT the period covered in the previous chapter, from the Han dynasty until the end of T'ang, the human figure occupied the same dominant position in Chinese painting as it did in pre-modern Occidental art. By the ninth century, however, the interest of artists had begun to shift from man to nature; by the eleventh century the shift was complete, and was never afterward reversed. It was landscape that was to prove the characteristic product and chief glory of the whole tradition.

Figure painting flourished primarily in a Confucian context; the rise of landscape painting, on the other hand, seems to have been stimulated by Taoist attitudes and ideas. The practice of seeking out places of scenic beauty, of "communing with nature," first became popular in a school of Taoist poets and painters of the Six Dynasties period. They dwelt upon their emotional responses to the sights and sounds of nature and were inspired by them to the creation of works of art, thus adding positive values to the negative attraction (freedom from human society) that the wilderness had held for the early Taoists. Earlier painters had used landscape as an adjunct to pictures of human activities; those of the fourth and fifth centuries began to depict it for its own sake.

In a short and enigmatic essay titled "Preface on Painting Landscape," one of these painters, Tsung Ping (375-443), relates that when old age came upon him and he grew too feeble to climb mountains, he re-experienced his former travels by painting the scenery of his memories on the walls of his room and gazing at these pictures. His essay is an affirmation of the power of painting to function as a substitute for the thing it represents, by arousing in the viewer those emotions that the actual scene would arouse. The forms of nature, he says, possess not only physical substance but also immaterial qualities of "attractiveness" or "flavor"; and it is by these qualities, rather than by outward appearances, that the spirit of the sensitive man is affected. If the artist is so affected himself and manages to transfer his feeling to his picture—if, as Tsung Ping puts it, he takes "response to his eyes and accord with his heart" as his guiding principle— then all other eyes will respond to, and all hearts be in accord with, his paintings. It is this concept which underlies the early landscape painting of China. The Sung dynasty writers' praise of landscape as "making one feel as if he were really in the place depicted" is a later reflection of the same idea.

No example of landscape painting survives from the age of Tsung Ping, but a copy of a scroll attributed to Ku K'ai-chih, illustrating a narrative poem titled *The Nymph of the Lo River*, offers some clue to its probable nature. The detail reproduced here represents the final scene of the poem, in which the poet, deserted by the river goddess after an abortive love affair, sits disconsolate on the bank of the river. The elements of the landscape—hills, rocks, trees—still preserve their character as images; conceived individually, they are juxtaposed as one would arrange ready-made stage props, without much concern for size relationships or placement in space. They serve to demarcate the separate episodes of the story, or to enclose the groups of figures that carry the narrative. The figures are disproportionately large, perhaps because the story is still the prime consideration of the painter. It is hard to imagine that such landscape, which is probably no more primitive than that envisioned by Tsung Ping when he composed his essay, could ever have inspired such an emotional response as the essay suggests. Neither the painter's technical means nor his power of visualization were adequate to suggest, at least to the modern viewer, the animistic world of Tsung Ping's text, in which plants, streams and rocks are endowed with spiritual essences and captivate the soul of man. Still less could he call forth any sense of the grand and pervasive movement which unites the Taoist cosmos into a single organism. That remained for landscapists of later centuries to achieve. But the viewer of a painting responds to familiar conventions with a directness denied to those who find them strange; the mushroom-like trees and modest hillocks of this naïvely presented scene were no doubt metamorphosed, in the eyes of the early nature-lover, into dense forests and towering peaks.

Far more impressive, although still preserving some residue of the archaic, is the landscape in the famous *Emperor Ming-huang's Journey to Shu*, believed to be a close copy of an eighth century design. The event depicted occurred in 756; Ming-huang, driven from the capital by a revolt, made the long journey southwest to Shu (modern Szechwan Province), following the rugged mountain road. The diagonally jutting crags, the road precariously propped out from a sheer cliff, the dark and mysterious clefts in the rocks, are intended to impart a sense of harshness and danger. Their effect is softened, however, by the brilliance of the pigments; it is hard to see any peril in a scene so cheerfully colored, so charmingly embroidered with flowering trees. The ancient and orthodox mode of painting in fine outline and heavy washes of color here reaches its culmination, achieving a richness which satisfies the T'ang love for lavish surfaces. In applying this technique to landscape, however, the artist found himself forced into some curious conventions, and severely hampered in the rendition of height and distance, mass and texture. He is limited to a world sharply defined and without shadows, made up of cleanly fractured rocks, hard-edged clouds, solitary trees and bushes. Nature is made unnaturally neat, and perceived with unnatural clarity.

Such an air of clarity and precision seems to imply a physical world susceptible to analysis by human intellect. The same firm confidence in the humanistic ideal that pervades T'ang figure painting is thus reflected even in landscape. But it was not to last. The revolt that drove the emperor Ming-huang into exile, even though it failed, signaled

Attributed to Ku K'ai-chih (born ç. 345), copy of the twelfth or thirteenth century:
The Nymph of the Lo River. Section of a handscroll. (H. 9½") Freer Gallery of Art, Washington, D.C.

the tragic fall from power of this most brilliant of dynasties, and put an end to the sense of security that permeates these pictures. It was during the following century that artists began to turn their attention away from the sphere of human affairs, now too obviously flawed with failure to merit the original faith. Nature, even in its most awesome and unfathomable aspects—and the tenth and eleventh century landscapists, more than their T'ang predecessors, were profoundly aware of these aspects—proved in the end the more rewarding to those in search of absolutes.

The heavily colored "blue-and-green" manner of landscape to which this picture belongs was already, by the late eighth century, a bit old-fashioned; more progressive painters were exploring the advantages of broader kinds of brushwork in place of the fine-line drawing, and of the reduction or complete exclusion of color. The famous poet-painter Wang Wei (699-759) is credited by later critics, perhaps undeservedly, with several innovations, including the *p'o-mo* or "broken ink" method, a means of "breaking"

Anonymous (eleventh century copy of an eighth century composition?): The Emperor Ming-huang's Journey to Shu.
Detail from a hanging scroll. Ink and colors on silk. Palace Museum Collection, Taichung.

by deeper-toned accents that flatness which can easily afflict ink-wash painting, and the use of *ts'un*, or texture strokes; both techniques were essential to the later evolution of the ink monochrome landscape. Other artists were carrying out more extreme forms of experimentation. We read of one eighth century master who spread silk on the floor and spattered ink freely onto it, then turned the result into a recognizable landscape by the addition of some brush lines. Another painted with a worn-out brush, still another with his own braided hair, dipped in ink. The prize for eccentricity must go to the painter who faced in one direction and painted in another, waving the brush in time to music. Most of these men worked while drunk, in a frenzy only partly aesthetic. Today's "action painters," when they claim Oriental precedents for their styles, are more right than they may realize. Those who indulged in such eccentricities were for the most part minor artists, but their unorthodox techniques, grouped under the *i-p'in* or "untrammeled class" of painting, were to have a profound effect on later styles. The authority of the traditional mode was broken.

The Five Dynasties period (906-960) which followed the T'ang was another era of political division; China was again split into small states ruled by short-lived dynasties. Several schools of landscape that were to continue into the Sung dynasty were inaugurated during this short but crucial period. The great landscapists of the Five Dynasties remain indistinct figures; it is perhaps too much to hope that any considerable number of authentic works from their hands will ever come to light, and the task of isolating their individual styles in existing copies and imitations remains to be done. Especially shadowy are the earliest of them, Ching Hao and Kuan T'ung, active in the late ninth and early tenth centuries. The creation of a more monumental landscape type, with a new sense of solidity in the rocks and mountains, was evidently their achievement. Later in the century, Tung Yüan and his pupil Chü-jan inaugurated an important school in the south, portraying the characteristic scenery of the area just below the Yangtze River. A few early paintings either by them or by close followers reveal their style more clearly. The typical productions of this school are river landscapes with rounded hills, drawn in a broad, relaxed manner, with a profusion of small dots and streaks of ink softening the forms and giving them an earthy texture.

The quest of the Five Dynasties and early Sung landscapists was for pictorial unification. The subordination or elimination of color was a move toward that end, since the tapestry-like variegation of early landscape had tended to fragment the composition. A new emphasis on brushwork gave surface consistency to the painting. Most important of all, methods were developed to create a spatial continuum within the picture: the use of concealing mists, the convincing depiction of recessions into depth, the drawing of distant objects in thinner tones of ink to suggest a hazy atmosphere. A landscape was no longer an assemblage of individual images, but set forth a coherent vision.

The painter who has been called the greatest of Chinese landscapists, Li Ch'eng, was active in the north during the late Five Dynasties and early Sung period. He specialized in winter scenes, perhaps because they agreed with something austere and wintry

Attributed to Li Ch'eng (tenth century), but probably eleventh century in actual date:
A Buddhist Temple in the Mountains. Detail from a hanging scroll. Ink and light color on silk.
William Rockhill Nelson Gallery of Art, Kansas City.

Fan K'uan (early eleventh century): Traveling among Streams and Mountains. Detail from a hanging scroll. Ink and light color on silk. Palace Museum Collection, Taichung.

in his personal nature, but also for reasons related to technique: the black-and-white scenery of this season was well suited to depiction in ink monochrome, and its bare trees, with their traceries of branches and twigs, served as ideal vehicles for displaying the extraordinary vitality of his brushwork. Li Ch'eng was regarded by his contemporaries as superhuman, sharing in the creative forces of nature. His influence on painting was profound. The grandeur of Northern Sung landscape, the supreme achievement of

Chinese painting, probably owes more to him than to any other single figure. Many of the finest surviving landscapes, notably those of Fan K'uan, Hsü Tao-ning and Kuo Hsi, are by men who acknowledged Li Ch'eng as their master.

The paintings attributed to Li himself all appear to be by lesser artists of later ages, but a few of them retain some trace of that stupendous creative power. *A Buddhist Temple in the Mountains*, probably painted around a century after the time of Li Ch'eng, is one of these. In the stillness of a mountain gorge, bare trees stand against thin mists. Those in the foreground are dark and distinct; further back, they fade to pale silhouettes. The very essentials of T'ang and earlier landscape, the warmth of color and charm of individualized details, are sacrificed to gain a new gravity of mood. The T'ang landscapist's presentation of nature as an assemblage of elements carefully analyzed and depicted no longer satisfies the Sung artist, who attempts to comprehend the physical world intuitively. His transformation of visual impressions into this superb coherence of form reveals his conviction of a coherence and order underlying surface appearances in nature, the same conviction that inspired Sung philosophers to erect the vast and orderly structure of the Neo-Confucian cosmology.

With Li Ch'eng we have arrived at the Sung dynasty (960-1279), the age of full maturity of Chinese painting. The first half of the dynasty, during which the capital was located at the northern city of K'ai-feng, is known as the Northern Sung period; the remainder after 1127, when the capital was moved to Hang-chou in the south, as the Southern Sung. For about a century and a half after the foundation of the dynasty, the empire was again united and relatively secure. A succession of artists of great originality and power produced masterworks which remained for later ages to admire, to emulate and to despair of equaling. Very few works by these men survive today, but those few give substance to the reverential appraisals they have received from all Chinese connoisseurs. The perfect balance between nature and art was attained in their works. Prodigious technique was applied to valid pictorial ends, never exploited in order to impress by sheer virtuosity; a classical restraint governed the expression, allowing no lapses into sentimentality. The artists approached nature as if for the first time, and responded to it with wonder and awe. The freshness of their vision and the depth of their understanding were never to be quite recaptured.

The supreme monument of the period is a large signed landscape by Fan K'uan, an early eleventh century master. He began his career by imitating the works of Li Ch'eng, but then, it is reported, came to a sudden realization: "My predecessor's method consisted of a direct apprehension of things in nature; here am I, learning from a man, which is not the equal of learning from the things themselves. But better than either of these methods is the way of learning from my own heart." Thereafter, we are told, he altered his style, and founded a school of his own. Like Li Ch'eng he is

Fan K'uan (early eleventh century): Traveling among Streams and Mountains. Hanging scroll. ▶
Ink and light color on silk. (61×29¼") Palace Museum Collection, Taichung.

credited by Sung critics with a power akin to that of natural creation; his works were endowed, that is, with the same all-pervading rightness or inherent order which one senses in natural scenery. Nature can never produce a rock or tree that looks artificial and wrong; an ordinary mortal can, but a truly great artist, the critics maintained, never will, because he works with the same spontaneity as nature itself, and without human willfulness.

Fan K'uan's one extant work, *Traveling among Streams and Mountains*, satisfies fully the expectations aroused by this praise. The composition is one of heroic simplicity, serene, free of trickery, showiness or any obvious trace of artifice. It is a vision so compelling that questions of subjectivity or objectivity, pursuit of likeness or the rejection of it, become irrelevant; the world of the painting seems neither to reflect faithfully the physical universe nor to overlay it with a human interpretation, but to have an absolute existence in itself. A massive bluff dominates the scene, its scale set by the trees and buildings on the crest of the knoll below. In a dark, mysterious cleft, a waterfall drops as a thin streak of white. Mists thrown up at its base drift through the valley, adding a further impression of soaring height to the cliff by obscuring its base. The quality of the drawing is best seen in the detail: the lineament, and particularly the thick, jagged contours of trees and rocks, is charged with an electric energy. The foliage of the trees is depicted by accumulation of individually delineated leaves, but in spite of all the labor involved in the method, the result has no air of laboriousness. The surfaces of boulders and cliffs are defined with texture strokes of the kind called by the Chinese "raindrop *ts'un*": innumerable small, pale-toned brushstrokes are applied to give a convincingly tactile rendering of the faces of rock. These technical devices, and such motifs as the scrubby foliage surmounting the bluff, were all to be imitated by later landscapists working "in the Fan K'uan manner"; they appear here in their pristine, unmannered forms. Few reminders of man and his works are to be seen: two tiny figures driving mules, a bridge, a half-hidden temple. The rest is untouched nature.

Sung Dynasty Landscape: The Middle Period

3

THE second half of the Northern Sung period, from the mid-eleventh century into the early twelfth, was an especially eventful age in Chinese painting. To understand all that happened then, one would have to take into account the activities of many separate schools and individual masters: traditionalists and innovators, archaists and eccentrics, academicians and amateurs, working in a bewildering variety of styles.

The foremost exponent of the landscape tradition of Li Ch'eng who was active at this time was Kuo Hsi. He distinguished himself not only as a painter but also as author of the most important Chinese treatise on landscape, in which he describes his methods and states his beliefs. Like Tsung Ping six centuries before, he maintained that the value of landscape painting lay in its capacity to make the viewer feel as if he were really in the place depicted. A genuine lover of the wilderness, he says, may be prevented by circumstances from carrying out his dreamed-of wanderings among mountains and streams; but he can experience imaginary journeys by gazing at paintings. The artist who would paint such landscapes must himself be intimate with mountains, observing their aspects in various kinds of weather, at different times of day and year. Mountains in spring are light and seductive, as if smiling; those in winter sad and tranquil, as if sleeping. All this is captured by the sensitive and skillful painter. "Contemplation of such pictures arouses corresponding feelings in the heart; it is as if one really came to these places. Herein lies the marvelous quality that paintings possess in addition to their (descriptive) meaning."

Kuo Hsi's masterwork, *Early Spring*, signed and dated to the year 1072, is the only other extant Chinese landscape that rivals the Fan K'uan painting in grandeur. But it is grandeur of a different sort, a turbulent vision of the world in flux rather than an affirmation of immutability in nature. The earth forms, swollen to an exaggerated rotundity, fuse and interpenetrate like parts of a vast organism. The strong sense of unrest that activates the picture is intensified by the use of a nervous, wavering line, constantly fluctuating in breadth, and the suggestion of an unnatural illumination, by which rocks can be lit from below, and shadows flicker mysteriously over a surface. Most unsettling of all is the regularity with which the ponderous masses are deeply undercut, as if by aeons of erosion. In what would seem to have been a last-minute

Kuo Hsi: Early Spring. Dated 1072. Hanging scroll. Ink and light colors on silk. (62¼×42½″)
Palace Museum Collection, Taichung.

change of plan, for example, the artist has altered what should have been the solid earth foundation for the pavilion at extreme right into a perilously overhanging ledge, and opened below a glimpse into a subterranean world. Something in the temperament of Kuo Hsi abhorred stability.

So much borders on fantasy; and yet when we move nearer to study the individual scenes in the cells of space enclosed by these coiling masses of earth and rock—the vista over an eroded river valley at left, the temple in a hazy gorge at right, boatmen disembarking on the shore in each of the lower corners—we find a degree of realism beyond anything encountered earlier. Kuo Hsi has brought to perfection the technique of atmospheric perspective, a method of creating the illusion of space and distance by depicting objects in progressively lighter tone as they recede into depth, suggesting the intervention of atmosphere between them and the viewer. Local areas of mist obscure

Attributed to Kuo Hsi: Autumn in the River Valley. Section of a handscroll. Ink and light colors on silk. (H. 10¼″) Freer Gallery of Art, Washington, D.C.

the tops of trees, and, as in the Fan K'uan landscape, increase the sense of height by masking the bases of the cliffs. That the profusion of detail does not weaken the coherence of the design is part of the wonder of the picture. Although each of the spidery bare trees is individually characterized, they serve by repetition as a unifying motive, and as a relief to the weightiness of the masses.

Of the many other works attributed to Kuo Hsi, a handscroll in the Freer Gallery, *Autumn in the River Valley*, agrees best with the *Early Spring* as a production of the same hand. The points of similarity are numerous, even though the handscroll is much smaller and quieter in mood. It answers the requirements set forth in Kuo Hsi's treatise, inviting the viewer to share in imagination the feelings of the strolling scholars who move leisurely through the landscape—one of them is seen approaching a rustic wine shop in the section reproduced. Since this is intended as "a painting one can move around in," a feeling of spaciousness is essential. Here as in the *Early Spring*, Kuo Hsi has created a hollow of space, using foreground rocks and tall pines for *repoussoir*. The cliffs and ridges are depicted in a softer manner, with pale contours or none at all, and a texture suggestive of crumbling earth. This is a technique suited to the smaller dimensions of the handscroll, but not to the huge hanging scroll, for which a firmer structure is required.

The Freer handscroll indicates that Kuo Hsi, who was an influential member of the Imperial Painting Academy, probably did much to introduce the new, more intimate mode that was to dominate landscape painting during the following two centuries; but anticipations of it can be found even earlier. In particular, the format and function of the handscroll, which is meant to be seen at close range, encouraged the artist to draw nearer to his subject. This close-up presentation can be observed as early as the tenth century, in the *River Journey at First Snowfall* scroll attributed to Chao Kan (p. 58), and again in a handscroll from the first half of the eleventh century with a similar title, *Clearing after Snow on the River*. The latter painting is signed by a less-known artist, Kao K'o-ming, and is dated 1035. Unrolling this scroll takes one on an imaginary journey along the river, past cottages of retired scholars, fishermen in their boats, bamboo groves and tall pines. The most poetic passage is near the end: a solitary fisherman, trudging homeward along the shore, crosses a clearing between groves of trees. A spot of bright color, he provides an effective foil for the greyed tones of the wintry landscape. Skillful use of atmospheric perspective, surrounding the nearby trees with haze and dimming those more distant, and a convincing recession along diagonally placed earth masses, open a deep space behind him. In the success with which this is accomplished, the painting seems advanced for its time, and in other ways as well: the broad broken sweeps of dilute ink on the heavily eroded banks, for example, resemble the "axe-cut" system of texture strokes used by Li T'ang more than a half-century later.

Li T'ang was the next major landscapist after Kuo Hsi in the Imperial Academy. He served the Emperor Hui-tsung at the northern capital of K'ai-feng during the last decades of the Northern Sung period, then followed the imperial court when it moved southward, under pressure from the Chin Tartars, to establish the new capital at Hang-chou, below the Yangtze River. He was over seventy at the time, and lived for less

Anonymous (eleventh or twelfth century): A Market Village by the River. Section of a handscroll.
Ink and light colors on paper. (H. 11¼″) Palace Museum Collection, Taichung.

than a decade after the move; but he managed to so dominate the newly reorganized
Painting Academy that there was scarcely a single Academy landscapist during the whole
of the Southern Sung period (1127-1279) who was not in some way his follower. Li T'ang
himself belonged in the tradition of Fan K'uan, sharing that master's fondness for
weathered rock cliffs surmounted by scrubby vegetation, and somber, shadowed gorges.
He painted monumental landscapes, at least one of which, a well-known work in the
Palace Museum collection dated 1124, is still extant. But the dimensions of the large

hanging scroll, ideally suited to the majestic visions of the Northern Sung painters, were less adaptable to the more intimate spirit that was now becoming popular. Li T'ang's achievements in the smaller forms, the handscroll and the album leaf, were probably at least as influential as his large-scale compositions.

The fan-shaped album leaf titled *A Myriad Trees on Strange Peaks*, although it carries an attribution to a much earlier artist, can be convincingly ascribed on grounds of style to Li T'ang. The trees in it are distinctively his, and the contours of the rocks; the rock surfaces are treated with a variant of his characteristic "axe-cut *ts'un*," a method derived from the "raindrop *ts'un*" of Fan K'uan but replacing the fine dabs of ink by broader sweeps, applied with the brush held in an inclined position. The resemblance of the resulting surface to that of a block of wood hewn with an axe accounts for the curious name. The use of the technique is difficult to see in this small picture; it appears more clearly, and in more mannered form, in the large dated landscape mentioned above. Passages strikingly similar to this album leaf in subject and style are to be seen in both the large landscape and a handscroll by Li T'ang in the same collection. They occur in these other paintings as subordinate elements, however; and the fact that Li T'ang has utilized what is essentially a detail from a large composition as the entire theme for a painting is itself significant: from the grand, all-inclusive vision, encompassing mountains, forests, rivers, buildings, paths—the painting as a world complete in itself—the artist's field of view narrows now to a small fragment of nature. More concentrated, the picture gains in immediacy. One no longer wanders in imagination through the scenery, pausing to enjoy individualized details, but instead absorbs at once the whole content of this cool, calm view of mysterious peaks rising above the fog. This may well be the earliest extant Chinese landscape that contains no stream or waterfall, no animals, no trace of human handiwork, nothing to break the absolute stillness. Mountains, trees and mists: only these, arranged and presented as a unified image. The painting attains by a drastic reduction of elements that coherence which Fan K'uan had achieved through more complex and difficult means of formal organization.

The feeling of spaciousness, noted already in the works of Kuo Hsi and Kao K'o-ming, is heightened by this reduction, and by the use of a compositional type which probably originated with Li T'ang, and became a favorite of Southern Sung landscapists. The picture is divided diagonally, with the entire foreground, containing the elements of greatest weight, compressed into the lower half. Li T'ang keeps a few peaks in the upper left segment; even these were to be all but eliminated in works by his followers. There is less of solid matter in the scene than there had been in earlier landscape, and it is made to seem still less by the expansion of the mists: no longer confined to the bases of cliffs and to the role of masking areas of difficult transition, they now flow freely between the peaks, and outward through the boundaries of the picture. A circumscribed view of a remote corner of the world, by drawing the imagination far beyond its actual limits, thus implies all the rest that lies outside it. This is no less a microcosm than the grand vistas of earlier centuries had been. The sense of vastness it conveys

Kao K'o-ming: Clearing after Snow on the River. Dated 1035. Detail from a handscroll.
Ink and colors on silk. (H. 16½") Collection of John M. Crawford, Jr., New York.

Probably by Li T'ang, early twelfth century (misleading attribution to Yen Wen-kuei, tenth to eleventh century):
A Myriad Trees on Strange Peaks. Album leaf. Ink and light colors on silk. (9¾×10¼″)
Palace Museum Collection, Taichung.

does not depend, as before, upon the depiction of lofty cliffs and deep recessions along river valleys, but purely upon the evocative use of space. The hazy void in which the peaks and trees are set becomes as significant, pictorially and expressively, as the forms themselves. The void, and the interrelationships of the rocky spires within it, are perceived intuitively; the picture is not constructed according to rational principles, least of all according to any such geometric formulae as underlie Occidental linear perspective. Once more, and in still another mode, the Chinese landscapist has succeeded in embodying in painting the organic cosmos of the Taoist and Neo-Confucian world view.

The main course of landscape in this period, the important schools and masters, the activities of the Academy, are fairly well understood; but there were, as always, artists who stood outside these relatively well-charted paths, working in individual manners, or continuing traditions of painting that had declined to the status of minor local phenomena. Their works, if unsigned, are difficult to place. One such problematic work is the short handscroll titled *A Market Village by the River*, which fits into no familiar category. It appears to be a production of the eleventh or twelfth century; if the latter, it is decidedly *retardataire*. There are suggestions of the Fan K'uan manner in the massive bluff at the left, and of the Tung Yüan school in the flat river bank and rounded distant hills at right. The landscape proper is of less importance, however, than the genre details in it, drawn meticulously in the finest of line. A trading junk approaches the shore, where three similar vessels are already moored, one displaying its occupants' laundry on a line strung from the mast. The riverside village is populated with lively figures: two travelers lunching in a restaurant, an old man chastising a servant who kneels before him, a boy driving a mule, a scholar climbing toward the temple in the valley above. A caravan of camels and their drivers, simply depicted in silhouette, is seen filing through the pass at right. The picture may represent a particular place, and perhaps there is some story connected with it; but these questions, like those of its date and authorship, remain as yet unanswered.

Figure Painting of the Five Dynasties and Sung

4

In the short and turbulent interim between the T'ang and Sung dynasties, while the five ephemeral powers that give the Five Dynasties period its name were succeeding one another rapidly in the Yellow River region, two more stable governments in the south, the Shu and the Southern T'ang, provided refuge for artists in search of peace and patronage. The Southern T'ang controlled most of what is known as the Chiang-nan area, south of the Yangtze, and had its capital at Nanking. It was ruled from 961 until 975, when it was finally absorbed into the Sung, by the famous poet-emperor Li Yü. He claimed descent from the imperial family of the T'ang dynasty, and considered his own dynasty as its legitimate successor. The dominant tone of Li Yü's court was one of elegance and aestheticism, and the painting created under the court patronage transmits something of that flavor. Figure painters in Li Yü's academy followed T'ang traditions. Especially popular were scenes of palace life in the manner of Chang Hsüan and Chou Fang; such sensitive portrayals of aristocratic pleasures and pastimes suited perfectly the taste that prevailed within this fragile enclave of culture.

Most famous of the Southern T'ang figure painters was Chou Wen-chü, who imitated Chou Fang, but, says a twelfth century catalog, "surpassed him in elegance and refinement." An unsigned and unattributed painting representing *A Palace Concert*, one of Chou Wen-chü's favorite subjects, has more likelihood of being a work of his period and school, if not of his hand, than any of those actually ascribed to him. The genre is familiar from T'ang painting. Four women, playing on the lute, cither, flute and mouth organ, accompanied by a servant who keeps time with wooden clappers, make up a chamber ensemble. Five others drink wine from celadon cups. They are already tipsy; one, at the far left, is supported by an attendant. Behind her is the empress, wearing an elaborate headdress and holding a flat fan; she alone preserves her dignity, sitting upright. The figures, although unmistakably based on those of Chou Fang, have lost something of the T'ang sense of volume. The long curves of the early style are replaced by sharp breaks, and the line itself fluctuates slightly in breadth here and there. If we leave aside these details of style, however, the picture might well persuade us (as it was meant to do) that nothing of importance had changed since the age of Chou Fang. The colors are still as bright and cheerful, the ladies as plump. The artist and his models

School of Chou Wen-chü (tenth century): A Palace Concert. Hanging scroll. Ink and colors on silk. (19⅛×27⅜″)
Palace Museum Collection, Taichung.

assume the same air of calm assurance, as if the T'ang had never fallen. Painters in the Nanking court must have done their part in maintaining Li Yü's precious illusion of perpetuating a glory long vanished.

Further west, in what is now Szechwan Province, the Shu state held out in a like way against the tumult of the time. Some artists who had served under the last T'ang emperors fled to Chengtu, the Shu capital, and a flourishing school of painting grew up there, a generally more progressive school than that of the Southern T'ang. From literary accounts, we know of the popularity in Shu of the *i-p'in* or "untrammeled" styles, and of ink monochrome. Two small pictures in Japan attributed to one of the Chengtu artists, Shih K'o, although they are much later than the Five Dynasties period in date, may be free copies after his works, and can give us some hint of how the rough brushwork of the *i-p'in* was applied to the painting of figures.

Since the subjects of the pictures pertain to Ch'an Buddhism (Japanese Zen), we must pause to consider that unique sect. The semi-legendary story of the transmission of Ch'an from India to China by Bodhidharma in the early sixth century is well known; but it need not prevent us from thinking of Ch'an as properly a Chinese product. Buddhism, centuries before, had converted a good part of China; now China converted Buddhism. The evolution of Ch'an to its maturity in the seventh and eighth centuries owed more to Taoism, and to a succession of Chinese thinkers, than to any foreign importation. This is no doubt one reason why Ch'an penetrated so deeply into the intellectual life of the late T'ang, Five Dynasties and Sung periods, and was the only sect to sustain its strength in the midst of a general Buddhist decline in China. In Ch'an, most of the appurtenances of orthodox Buddhist sects—ritual, the pantheon of deities, holy images, the scriptures—are denied any real value. All these are regarded, in fact, as obstacles to the attainment of individual enlightenment, and are rejected in favor of a direct assault on that goal. Ratiocination leads away from it, intuition toward it, ever closer, until some shock—it can even be physical—accomplishes the final break-through.

The fact that the rise to popularity of the new painting styles, including the rough manners of brushwork and ink monochrome, was contemporary with the popularization of Ch'an, may be responsible for the often-encountered exaggerations of the closeness of relationship between the two movements. Ch'an was no more responsible for ink monochrome painting than it was for Ch'an; the new styles were employed by Ch'an artists, but also (and earlier) by Confucian literati, Taoist recluses, and the masters of landscape about whose broader beliefs we know nothing at all. There is no reason to suppose that Shih K'o was personally committed to Ch'an; he painted Taoist, orthodox Buddhist and secular subjects as well.

The *Two Patriarchs Harmonizing their Minds* ascribed to Shih K'o, however, are unmistakably Ch'an personages. One of them leans comfortably upon the back of a tiger, his head lowered between hunched shoulders. Whether he is meditating or asleep is uncertain; the tiger, in any case, is asleep. Something other than an ordinary hair brush, probably a brush of straw or shredded bamboo, has been employed in drawing the garment of the man and the fur of the tiger. The experience of such a picture is quasi-kinesthetic. One senses, in observing these ragged lines, the vigorous movements of the painter. Where his brush rested momentarily, blots of deep black remain; where it moved more swiftly, streaks of ink trailed behind it as the fibers of the brush separated. The man's face and the tiger's mask are finished with more conventional strokes. This manner of painting matches literary descriptions of Shih K'o's style, and belongs to the *i-p'in* tradition in its violent rejection of orthodox fine-line-and-color-wash technique. With its air of spontaneity, it suited the needs of Ch'an, and the future development of Ch'an painting lay chiefly in successive transformations of the "untrammeled" styles.

The orthodox sects of Buddhism, meanwhile, continued to commission icons in the traditional manners. Although their doctrines played no significant part in the main intellectual currents of the Sung period, except insofar as they influenced Neo-Confucian thought, they retained some popular following, and enough force to inspire an abundance

Anonymous: Portrait of the Ch'an Master Wu-chun. Dated 1238. Detail from a hanging scroll. Ink and colors on silk. Tōfukuji, Kyoto.

of painting, ranging in quality from indifferent to excellent. The entire range is represented among surviving works, especially in the rich collections of Japanese temples. Most of the paintings are unsigned; the artists were not famous, and their identity was of no special concern to purchasers of their works, who required objects for worship rather than for aesthetic enjoyment. The painters, accordingly, were not encouraged to develop individual styles; they tended to follow old models for their designs, and worked in whatever manner was orthodox in their time. They were constrained to iconographic correctness, and aimed at portraying the Buddhist subjects with skill and conviction, endowing them with whatever aspects were required: fierceness, benevolence, asceticism or nobility.

Anonymous, thirteenth century? (copy after Shih K'o?, tenth century): Patriarch and Tiger.
Detail from one of a pair of hanging scrolls representing Two Patriarchs Harmonizing their Minds. Ink on paper.
Commission for the Protection of Cultural Properties, Tokyo.

Anonymous (eleventh century): The Peacock King. Detail from a hanging scroll.
Ink and colors on silk. Ninnaji, Kyoto.

K'ung-chiao Ming-wang, the Peacock King, is represented in a superb early painting, one of the treasures of the Ninnaji, a Buddhist temple in Kyoto. Like many other deities of esoteric Buddhism, he is austere in appearance but benevolent in function: he devours the evil thoughts and passions which befoul the minds of humans, just as his peacock vehicle (in legend, at least) consumes poisonous snakes, insects and plants.

Chang Sheng-wen: Śākyamuni Buddha Preaching.
Painted in the period 1173-1176. Section of a long handscroll of Buddhist images. Ink and colors on paper. (H. 12″)
Palace Museum Collection, Taichung.

The two faces at the sides of his head have fierce expressions, while the central face is impassive. Probably Northern Sung in date, the picture is unsurpassed in beauty among surviving Buddhist paintings. The colors, bright mineral pigments, are well preserved, although the designs in gold line which originally covered the textiles have all but disappeared. The great fan-shaped tail of the peacock surrounds the deity like a second aureole. All this visual richness could easily have fallen into trivial decoration; instead, together with the quality of the drawing and the sense of power in tranquillity conveyed by the hieratic image, it lifts the painting to the level of the sublime.

The continuity of orthodox Buddhist styles may be seen in the similarities between the eighth century composition from Tun-huang (p. 10) and a twelfth century treatment of the same or a closely related subject which is part of a long handscroll of Buddhist images in the Palace Museum. An inscription on this latter painting is dated 1180, and identifies the artist as one Chang Sheng-wen, an otherwise unknown painter who worked far in the southwest, in the present province of Yünnan. It is painted on paper, in line of the utmost delicacy and subtle shades of color. The perfection of drawing, the refinement of the faces, sets Chang far above the anonymous image-makers of Tun-huang in skill and sensitivity. His strength apparently lay in these, however, and not in originality; or, if he was in fact endowed with any inventiveness, he was not encouraged to exercise it. The four guardian kings in the lower corners of the composition look as if they had been transmitted, without much change, from the Buddhist art of the T'ang dynasty; the Buddha and Bodhisattvas are likewise direct descendants of those in T'ang painting. We see here the end-product of a slow and natural evolution, with nothing of the conscious archaism practiced by other Sung painters. To some extent, the style has been brought up to date: the faces have the same gentleness, the drapery the same elaboration of festoons and ribbons, as we know from Sung sculpture. But so little significant change in five centuries bespeaks a backward-looking art, as most Buddhist painting of the Sung period certainly was.

Such pictures as these played no part in the Ch'an sect; its attitude toward cult images and holy texts is vividly displayed in some portrayals of famous Ch'an masters using images of the Buddha for firewood and ripping scriptures to shreds. All that can be transmitted must pass directly from one human being to another, from mind to mind. Anecdotes of the doings and sayings of masters of the past were of value in preserving some record of their individual insights. Portraits were painted for a similar reason; the relationship between master and pupil was very close, and a portrait of the master could recall that relationship to the pupil after he had left the monastery at the end of his apprenticeship. Several such portraits are preserved in temples in Japan, brought back from China by Japanese monks who went there to study.

The best of these, and perhaps the finest extant Chinese portrait, has for its subject the Ch'an master Wu-chun. It was painted by an anonymous artist; Wu-chun himself has inscribed it and written the date, 1238. According to this dedicatory inscription, the picture was done as a farewell present for the Japanese priest Ikkoku, who on his return to Japan founded the Tōfukuji, the Kyoto temple in which the painting is still

Li Sung: The Knick-knack Peddler. Dated 1210. Album leaf. Ink and light colors on silk. (10⅛×10⅞″)
Palace Museum Collection, Taichung.

kept. Wu-chun is portrayed seated in an alert pose, dressed in richly colored robes. It is the face, however, which commands attention: benign, eyes wide open, good humor evident in the wrinkles at the corners of the eyes and in the slight smile. A light modeling, with blushes of red along contours, gives it a surprisingly naturalistic look. Portraiture may have gone even further in the direction of realistic portrayal in the Sung period, but nothing else so far advanced as this survives.

Figure painters in the Imperial Academy, meanwhile, devoted themselves chiefly to secular themes: incidents from history and legend, illustrations to the classics, occasionally genre subjects; the last were especially common in the Southern Sung period. Li Sung, whose specialty was the careful delineation of architecture called in Chinese *chieh-hua* or "boundary painting," sometimes applied the same meticulous technique to representations of figures, producing such astonishing displays of draftsmanship as *The Knick-knack Peddler*. This is a fan-shaped album leaf, only about ten inches tall, with a signature and the date 1210. The painter has written on it, in addition, three tiny characters meaning "Five Hundred Articles," referring with well-justified pride to the number of individual objects he has drawn in the peddler's pack. The fineness of the drawing is not the only virtue of the picture; such lively pieces of characterization as the sly glances of the children and the patient expression of the harassed mother, such well-observed detail as the baby who reaches out for a toy without pausing from his suckling, make the painting more than a mere virtuoso showpiece.

Figures in Landscape and Garden Settings

5

T HE ever-changing dialogue between man and nature, in which man transforms his surroundings in imagination and is himself transformed by them, has been a lasting concern of poets and painters in China as elsewhere. The anonymous authors of the earliest Chinese poetry, the lyrics in the Chou dynasty *Book of Odes* (c. 800-600 B.C.), begin already to suggest some affinity in feeling between the human and non-human worlds, introducing plant, animal and other images from nature as a prelude to the statement of somehow congruent emotions. Early painters seem to have followed the pattern set by the poets, using a simple kind of evocative juxtaposition. In the *Nymph of the Lo River*, attributed to Ku K'ai-chih (p. 27), images of trees and hills, placed beside those of persons playing out their roles in the story, serve not so much to provide a convincing setting as to create a structure of mood into which the feelings of the human participants interweave. One senses this in the picture, even though the emotional associations of these images now communicate themselves to us only faintly.

It is tempting to suppose that the painter of the *Emperor Ming-huang's Journey to Shu*, the eighth century composition introduced previously in connection with T'ang dynasty landscape, was still using the same device, intending the harsh patterns of fractured rock with which he surrounds his principal figures to accord with the bitterness of the exiled and bereaved emperor. But it is more likely that this was simply his standard manner of depicting rocks, and would have been used in any case. The colorfulness of the scene, with bright-leafed trees and a scattering of flowers, would rather suggest a pleasure outing. The landscape assumes here a semi-independent status, and is not made to comment upon the narrative, or even to harmonize with it. It commands at least as much attention as the figure groups it encloses, but also serves as a stage for their actions: clefts in the mountains, tree-ringed glades, are carefully located so that the players may enter, perform and exit in the most orderly manner. In the lower right corner of the picture, a party of riders is seen filing through a narrow pass into an open area on the bank of a stream. It is the emperor himself who leads—he is identified by his princely bearing, and by the three tufts of hair into which the mane of his horse is tied. Four courtiers and seven palace ladies make up his retinue. He approaches a wooden bridge, which connects this compartment of the picture to the adjacent one.

Attributed to Chao Yen (tenth century): Eight Riders in Spring. Hanging scroll (cropped at top and bottom). Ink and colors on silk. (w. 40⅛″) Palace Museum Collection, Taichung.

Anonymous (eleventh century copy of an eighth century composition?): The Emperor Ming-huang's Journey to Shu.
Detail from a hanging scroll. Ink and colors on silk. Palace Museum Collection, Taichung.

Attributed to Chao Kan (tenth century): A River Journey at First Snowfall. Section of a handscroll.
Ink and colors on silk. (H. 10⅛″) Palace Museum Collection, Taichung.

Innovations in landscape during the Five Dynasties and early Sung period, bringing various solutions to the problem of creating a unified space within the picture, opened alternatives to this space-cell mode of construction. The so-called "level distance" composition, a method of presenting an unbroken view over a flat expanse of land or water, was perfected by such tenth century masters as Li Ch'eng and Tung Yüan. It is used effectively in a scroll attributed to Chao Kan, one of the painters who served with Tung Yüan in the Nanking academy. The scroll, titled *A River Journey at First Snowfall*, has been credited to Chao Kan since the early twelfth century, when it was recorded in the catalog of the Emperor Hui-ts'ungs collection. The author of that catalog comments on the evocative power of Chao Jan's river scenery: "Even though you may be among all the petty distractions of court or marketplace, you have only to look at it to be transported at once to the river." Eight centuries later, the painting preserves the same power. Unrolling the scroll, moving over this bleak stretch of grey water, among the sharp-cut islets, one is made to feel empathically the chill of the fishermen in their hovels and boats. Two of them huddle on a fishing platform raised on stilts, protected only by a mat covering from the wind that ruffles the surface of the river and bends the tassels of reeds. In the open water beyond, a punt goes by, poled by two boatmen, carrying colorfully dressed travelers. Snow is depicted with white pigment spattered lightly over the surface of the silk. The bunches of reeds, the islets, the boat, are all set off sharply by the surrounding ink wash, with a sense of isolation that enhances the lonely mood of the scene, as well as emphasizing the sparse, very sophisticated placing of elements within the area of the painting.

This mastery of arranging forms on a surface, and the unfailing sense of correct proportion in laying out the space around and between them, is the heritage of T'ang painting. It can be admired also in a large composition of about the same period representing *Eight Riders in Spring*. In order that the group of horsemen may be displayed with the utmost clarity, indications of setting have been kept few and simple. A balustrade marks the further limit of the scene, which is a palace courtyard. In a corner formed by a jog in this balustrade stand two trees, an ornamental rock and a short palm. Seven mounted noblemen encircle an eighth—the emperor?—who raises his whip. The drawing is crisp and admirable throughout, the coloring brilliant. For a picture of this age and size to have been preserved in such condition is an almost incredible piece of good fortune. But nothing in it contradicts the tenth century date traditionally assigned to it. The artist to whom it is ascribed, Chao Yen, was the son-in-law of an emperor of one of the Five Dynasties, and a leading collector and patron of art, besides painting himself. Like collector-painters in later times, he was fond of working in old styles. "On leisure days," writes a twelfth century historian, "he would usually set himself the task of completing some scroll in imitation of a well-known work by an old master." Perhaps it is such a picture that we have here. In any event, the hand that produced it was endowed with an antique elegance quite worthy of Chao's reputation.

The unknown painter of the picture titled *Breaking the Balustrade*, probably an artist of the Imperial Academy working in the twelfth century, has constructed a more elaborate setting for his drama. He is illustrating an edifying anecdote from history, concerned with the Han emperor Ch'eng-ti, his loyal minister Chu Yün, and the marquis Chang Yü. Chu Yün's indignation against the traitorous marquis overcame his prudence, the story goes, and he asked permission to wield the imperial sword to put him to death. The emperor, outraged by this unprecedented request, commanded instead that Chu himself be beheaded, but Chu clung to a balustrade and asked to be cut open on the spot, as another loyal servitor had once been executed. The emperor was impressed by Chu's

Anonymous (twelfth century?): Breaking the Balustrade. Hanging scroll (cropped at top and bottom).
Ink and colors on silk. (w. 40″) Palace Museum Collection, Taichung.

strength of purpose, and by the pleas of another minister, Hsin Ch'ing; he relented, canceled the death sentence for Chu, and ordered that the balustrade, broken in the scuffle, be left unrepaired as a memorial to the event.

Inanimate objects are here made to participate in the drama, to echo the play of passions between the four chief actors. The trunk and branches of a tall pine frame the main group at right, which has the emperor as its center. Two ornamental stones, pitted and hollowed by erosion, stand behind the two groups, reinforcing the impression of steadfast determination created by the figures themselves. Hsin Ch'ing stands isolated, forward of the others; Chang Yü cringes at the emperor's side. As in T'ang dynasty designs, the postures of the figures and their interrelationship in space are among the artist's chief means of characterization. So skillfully is it accomplished that we might guess what is happening without knowing the story; the tension of the moment is unmistakable. The total success of the picture as narrative, the success of the drawing in combining liveliness with precision, make of this one of the finest of Chinese figure compositions.

Anonymous (twelfth century?): "The Tribute Horse" (The Emperor Ming-huang's Journey to Shu?). Detail from a hanging scroll. Ink and colors on silk. Metropolitan Museum of Art, New York.

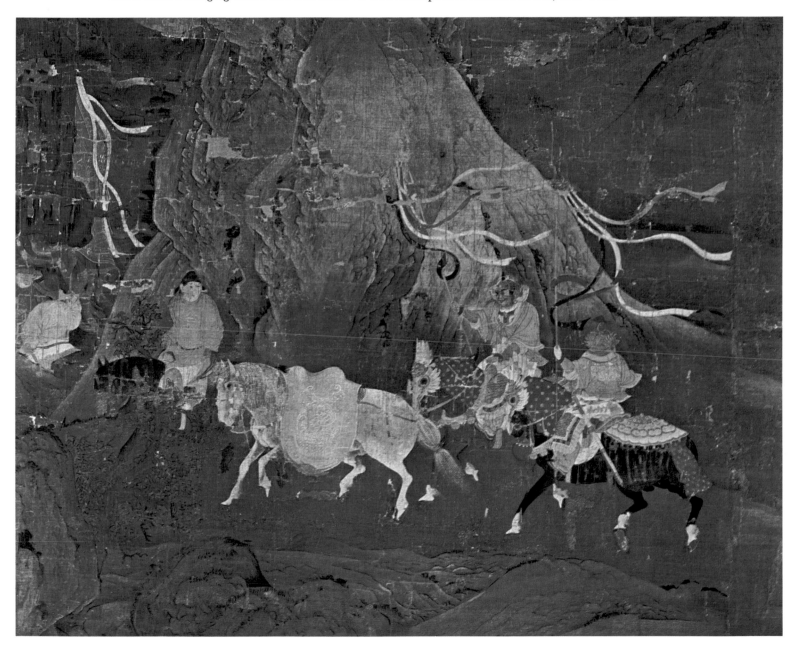

A work close to it in style, and rivaling it in splendor of color and refinement of drawing, is the well-known painting in the Metropolitan Museum of Art which has been called *The Tribute Horse*, but which may in fact be another representation of *The Emperor Ming-huang's Journey to Shu*. A mounted figure not shown in our detail has been said to represent Ming-huang. If this interpretation is correct, the riderless white horse alludes to the absence of the imperial consort Yang Kuei-fei, put to death at an earlier stage in the journey, and the somberness of the setting takes on new meaning. The rich blue, green, crimson and rose hues of the costumes and saddle-cloths have softened over the centuries, and the drawing in powdered gold on the trappings is worn and subdued, but the colors still glow brilliantly against the deep-toned silk ground. Washes of gold on the cliff face above the white horse give a strange luminosity to that part of the picture; it is as if the men and horses were emitting a mysterious light as they pass through the darkened landscape.

In paintings of the early periods, men move through nature as travelers, or pursue their private concerns in the midst of the most awesome or entrancing scenery. Even when subject to the harshness of an uncongenial environment, as are the fishermen in the Chao Kan scroll, they preserve some measure of self-containment. Nature is outside them and beyond their control. The poet seated on the river-bank in the *Nymph of the Lo River* scroll broods upon his personal tragedy, affected only unconsciously by his surroundings. The same is true of the figure in the anonymous eleventh century *Noble Scholar under a Willow*. The personage represented is probably the fourth century poet T'ao Yüan-ming, who retired from official life to enjoy the pleasures of the country, and became for later ages the ideal scholar-recluse. He sits on a leopard skin rug in a relaxed posture, his head sunk between his shoulders. On the ground before him are a bowl of wine, from which he has been drinking, and a scroll of paper, blank to receive the poem taking form in his mind. The face is pensive, the eyes narrowed in thought; it is an expression of inwardness. The curving willow that encloses the figure only increases this air of introspection. The willow, in China, is symbolic of sensual elegance (the sterner virtues belong to the pine and bamboo); here, it mirrors the poet's mood of aesthetic inebriation. Still, it is the artist who employs natural objects as a commentary on his subject; it is not the subject himself who willed them there.

In painting of the twelfth and thirteenth centuries, especially in the court Academy works of that period, a new attitude toward nature becomes apparent, one closer to Occidental romanticism. Those scenes once considered in the West to be most typical of Chinese painting, which portray scholars seated on mountain ledges gazing at water-falls or into mysterious voids, are products of this age and the new attitude. The type was created by the late twelfth century academy landscapist Ma Yüan, and imitated by his numerous followers. One of the finest surviving specimens of it is by his son Ma Lin, a large signed painting titled *Listening to the Wind in the Pines*.

The experience of being emotionally moved by the stimuli of nature, which in Six Dynasties art theory was considered to enrich the expressive content of a work of art, now becomes itself the subject of the work of art. It is presented as a cultivated

Anonymous (eleventh century?): A Noble Scholar under a Willow. Hanging scroll. Ink and colors on silk.
(25¾×15¾″) Palace Museum Collection, Taichung.

Ma Lin: Listening to the Wind in the Pines. Seal with the date 1246.
Hanging scroll (cropped at top and bottom). Ink and colors on silk. (w. 43½″) Palace Museum Collection, Taichung.

pastime, determinedly pursued. The aesthetic scholar of this picture, too self-conscious to enjoy the true relaxation of the drunken poet in the other, sits in a tense posture, striking a listening pose, with a sideward glance directed at his boy attendant. The elegant lines of the rocks, stream and distant mountains, the consummate refinement of form in the pine tree, belong to a world which exists within his mind; he is surrounded, in the picture, not by nature itself but by a projection of his emotional response to it. The ancient dialogue between man and the world, now that both sides are dictated by man himself, has become a soliloquy.

Bird, Flower and Animal Painting of the Sung Dynasty

6

THE Chinese critics customarily divide painting into three large subject-categories: the two dealt with in the previous chapters, figures and landscape, and a third which includes pictures of flowers and other plants, birds, insects and animals. Pictures in this third category were never taken so seriously by the critics, who tended to dismiss them as trivial. But they were no less popular for that, and occupied a surprising number of first-rank artists from the T'ang through the Sung periods. We read of bird and flower specialists in the T'ang dynasty, but know next to nothing about how they painted. What we have of this genre from T'ang is limited to decorative details in outdoor scenes, both Buddhist and secular. Blossoming trees, leafy bushes, small flowers, are interspersed among the figures in many of the wall paintings at Tun-huang, and in such landscapes as the *Emperor Ming-huang's Journey to Shu*. They enrich the picture surface, fill out the setting, and often indicate the season of the year. Neatly drawn, with different plants accurately distinguished, they lead one to conjecture that decorative beauty and representational accuracy were the aims of T'ang flower, bird and animal painting.

Just these qualities are most conspicuous in a famous pair of hanging scrolls in the Palace Museum collection, which represent herds of deer in an autumn forest of maple trees. They may originally have formed parts of a single, much larger composition, perhaps a screen. Something of T'ang style is undoubtedly preserved in them, but it is difficult to say how much, or in what features, since nothing really comparable survives from T'ang. There is, in fact, nothing else quite like them in the whole of Chinese painting. A convincing theory is that they were produced under the Liao dynasty of the Khitan Tartars, which controlled the north of China, along with parts of Mongolia and Manchuria, during the tenth and eleventh centuries. Wall paintings in the eleventh century Liao tombs at Ch'ing-ling, similar in subject but much cruder in execution, appear to represent a debasement of this same style, so the tenth century attribution usually given the Palace Museum pictures is quite reasonable. However we may account for it, there is something foreign in them; the decorative brocade of the autumn foliage, and the unusually naturalistic portrayal of the deer, have reminded some observers of Near Eastern painting. Fairly strong shading on the animals increases their plasticity without obscuring the skill and sensitivity of the linear drawing.

Anonymous (tenth century): Deer among Red-leafed Maples. Detail from a hanging scroll. Ink and colors on silk. Palace Museum Collection, Taichung.

Anonymous (early twelfth century?): Birds in a Thicket of Bamboo and Plum. Detail from a hanging scroll. Ink and colors on silk. Palace Museum Collection, Taichung.

It was the genius of the early Chinese painter that he could, when he wished, avoid giving any impression of intruding upon his subjects, portraying animals absorbed in their private activities and unaware of being observed. The effect of such paintings is that same sense of revelation of a world totally unfamiliar to us, remote from human concerns, which some films of animals made with concealed cameras and telescopic lenses have achieved in our own time. The feeling of mystery in a little-known early composition in the Palace Museum titled *Monkeys and Horses* arises in part from this alien quality, but also from the indeterminate character of the subject: what is the relationship, if any, between the monkeys, two of them hanging from the upper branches of a tree and a third perched on a rock, and the two horses below, trotting toward an undefined destination? If the painting ever carried any symbolic meaning, it has been forgotten, and the painter adds no clarifying comment, but only presents his curious scene with a matter-of-fact air. The monkeys are not turned into comical beasts, or the horses into unnaturally noble ones. The picture is attributed to an eighth century painter of horses, Han Kan, but appears to be later, probably Five Dynasties or early Sung in date. It is roughly contemporary with the *Deer among Red-leafed Maples*, then, but belongs firmly in an unmixed, native Chinese tradition. The rocks and trees, more than the animals, give a clue to the date; they appear to be prototypes of those seen in copies and imitations of tenth century paintings. Forms are given convexity by the simple device of shading along contours, with curved strokes on the tree trunks to establish their cylindrical shape. No texture strokes *(ts'un)* are used on the stone surface; some such use of graded washes as this must lie behind the "rocks like clouds" which critics admired in the landscapes of Li Ch'eng and Kuo Hsi.

The greatest master of bird-and-flower painting in the Northern Sung period was Ts'ui Po, a brilliant and independently-inclined member of the Imperial Academy. He dazzled his contemporaries by his practice of dispensing with preliminary sketches in charcoal, attacking the silk directly with the brush; he could draw long straight lines without using a straightedge, and his power of invention was inexhaustible. The painting which is probably his only surviving work, a large composition signed and dated to the year 1061, upholds his reputation, displaying just the combination of skill and spontaneity which the Sung writers praise. With a technical virtuosity matching that of his contemporary Kuo Hsi, he depicts the dead, windblown leaves, the bent reeds and bamboo in fine line and color washes, the tree with a dry, rough texture, the earth bank in broad strokes of ink. The aloofness of the tenth century masters has relaxed, and the artist penetrates with sympathetic understanding into the lives of his subjects. Two magpie jays, chattering at a bewildered hare, are admirably caught in mid-motion. The seemingly unstudied arrangement of these forms against a thin wash of ink, rendering the bleak winter sky, shares the naturalness of the best Northern Sung landscape.

Anonymous (tenth century?), attributed to Han Kan (eighth century): Monkeys and Horses. ►
Hanging scroll (cropped at top). Ink and colors on silk. (w. 19″) Palace Museum Collection, Taichung.

Emperor Hui-tsung: Two Finches on Twigs of Bamboo. Section of a handscroll. Ink and colors on silk. (H. 12¼")
Collection of John M. Crawford, Jr., New York.

◄ Ts'ui Po: Hare and Jays. Dated 1061. Hanging scroll (cropped at bottom). Ink and colors on silk. (W. 40¾")
Palace Museum Collection, Taichung.

Like landscape, however, bird-and-flower painting followed a different course from the late eleventh century, replacing this seemingly extemporaneous approach with one which gave greater value to precision and orderly arrangement. A major role in the shift in taste was played by the Emperor Hui-tsung (ruled 1101-1125), who was himself a bird-and-flower painter of major rank. The court Academy, under his patronage and active control, enlisted many of the leading artists of the age and rose to a dominance which it maintained until the fall of the dynasty. Hui-tsung's passion was for literal renderings of the real appearances of things; he reprimanded his painters for the most trivial lapses from accuracy. "Painters are not to imitate their predecessors," proclaimed a regulation issued to the Academy at the beginning of his reign, "but are to depict objects as they exist, true to form and color." Under the pressure of such demands, the painters might have fallen into the worst academicism, but they did not. The essence of the Academy style in Hui-tsung's time is not a photographic fidelity to nature at all; nature does not bound her creations with such elegant line, or dispose them in such exquisite, timeless arrangements. It is rather a crystalline clarity, a sense of perfection ideally achieved. These pellucid visions are derived closely from nature, but set forth with such absolute assurance as to create their own, separate reality. This, states the painter, is precisely how a pigeon or a branch of flowering plum looks, and no one would dare to doubt him.

Such an enchanting performance as the anonymous *Birds in a Thicket of Bamboo and Plum*, for example, if accepted on its own terms, makes even the masterwork of Ts'ui Po seem a bit artless and arbitrary. It is probably from the hand of some member of Hui-tsung's Academy, and may well be the only large-scale work by any of them to survive. Details in it are drawn with the same near-miraculous refinement which we know from the best album leaves of the school, and the same sense of order and clarity prevails in the composition—this in spite of the intricate overlapping of stalks of bamboo, branches of blossoming plum and tall briers, which should produce an impression of tangled confusion, but instead functions as an openwork screen upon which the birds are displayed. The arrangement is static, unlike that of Ts'ui Po, and no relationship is implied between the birds; they perch in isolation, in their assigned places. Minute and patient observation lies behind the visual truthfulness of individual elements—the artist understands how bamboo puts forth leaves and twigs, the difference between the sleek plumage of doves and the spiky feathers of the quail. But it is Ts'ui Po's picture which, in the end, better fulfills the purpose of bird-and-flower paintings stated in Hui-tsung's own catalog. Associated with the various creatures and plants of nature, says the author of that catalog, are ideas and emotions: rustic tranquillity with the quail, autumnal melancholy with deer, and so forth. "When these are presented in painting, they serve to evoke human thoughts. Such pictures not only capture the appearance of created things, but also transmit their essential spirit. They take hold of one's mind, as if one had come to the very place and were gazing at the thing itself." The passage is similar to one quoted previously from Kuo Hsi's treatise on landscape; both are expressions of the orthodox Chinese view of painting.

Several dozen pictures exist which are ascribed to Hui-tsung himself; most of them are signed with his famous illegible cipher; all but a few are patently imitations, and there is none at all which is entirely above controversy. One of the three or four most likely candidates, and one of the best in quality, is the short handscroll representing two small finches on twigs of bamboo growing from an overhanging bank. The arrangement of the birds, one in profile, the other facing forward but with its head turned to the side, was a favorite of Hui-tsung and his court painters, and appears in others of their compositions—for example, the pair of jays in the *Birds in a Thicket of Bamboo and Plum*. The two pictures agree also in their mode of presentation: the branches and twigs spread out in a single plane, like ribs of a fan; the birds perched primly upon

Anonymous, twelfth century (misleading attribution to Chao Ch'ang): A Branch of White Jasmine. Album leaf. Ink and colors on silk. (9¾×10⅛″) Sugahara Collection, Kamakura (Japan).

these; the earth banks drawn in contour and wash only, with no rendering of texture on the main areas. Whatever the respective ages and proper attributions of these two pictures may be, the relationship between them probably reflects accurately the relationship between the painter-emperor and his academy: the style of the Hui-tsung handscroll is a simplification of the style of the professional's composition, with technical requirements reduced to accommodate the sensitive and capable amateur.

The death of Hui-tsung, the removal of the imperial court to Hang-chou in the south and the drastic decline in Chinese power do not seem to have discomposed the Academy painters seriously. Under the reigns of Hui-tsung's son and grandson they continued, with the special imperturbability of bird-watchers in any age, to portray their small subjects with the same careful elegance. Along with the Southern Sung landscapists who were their contemporaries in the Academy, they seem to drift away from the imperfect, material world into an ideal realm, leaving behind the firm foundation in reality upon which Northern Sung painting had been built, and sometimes even the persuasive semblance of reality of Hui-tsung's painting circle. Their mood was milder, their aims more modest; what we have of their work consists almost entirely of album leaves, a form which they especially favored.

The exquisite *Branch of White Jasmine* in the Sugahara collection, although traditionally ascribed to an early eleventh century flower painter, belongs completely to the Southern Sung period in style and taste, and is probably by some twelfth century Academy master. Chao Ch'ang, the artist to whom it is attributed, was a conservative, working in a careful, relatively realistic manner; he referred to his pictures as *hsieh-sheng*, "transcriptions from life." Sung writers tell of his strolling in the garden early in the morning, holding flowers in his hand to draw them. It is not difficult to understand how his name became attached to such pictures as the Sugahara leaf. The precise depiction of leaves curling in space, the calculation and balancing of the weight of leaves and blossoms on the slender twigs, are accomplished with such assurance as to give an initial impression of a portrayal directly from life. It is only afterward that one becomes aware of the degree of idealization in the drawing. The diagonally divided composition, familiar from twelfth century landscape album-leaves, suggests the real date of the picture.

The Imperial Academy of the Southern Sung, like Li Yü's academy at the Southern T'ang court two centuries earlier, served an uneasy aristocracy that was forever looking northward in fear of invasion. Painters working in such times felt, perhaps, the need to affirm the values of peace and stability. In scenes of palace ladies in protected courtyards, of children playing in gardens, of scholars in mountain seclusions so well tended as to seem corners of the park, a sunlit tranquillity excluded all hint of cold, barbarian wind from the north. Even bird and animal pictures of the Southern Sung academy share in this mood. It permeates two small paintings attributed to the twelfth century Academy artist Mao I, one of a bitch and puppies, the other of a mother cat and kittens, both in garden settings. The mother cat, in its plump haughtiness, is an animal counterpart of T'ang court ladies; the same aristocratic conviction of security is expressed in

Attributed to Mao I (twelfth century): Mother Cat and Kittens in a Garden. Album leaf.
Ink and colors on silk. (10×10⅜″) Yamato Bunka-kan, Osaka.

its poise and calm gaze. Two of the kittens wrestle playfully. Another, in the foreground, its orange fur all but invisible against the brown silk, gazes upward at a pair of small, white butterflies dancing in the air beside the hollyhocks.

Landscapes of the Southern Sung Academy
Ma Yüan, Hsia Kuei, Ma Lin

7

WHEN, after some unsettled years, the Sung capital was finally established at Hang-chou in 1138, the imperial court came into new surroundings, the luxuriant terrain of the region known as Chiang-nan, literally "South-of-the-River," i.e. of the Yangtze. Under the spell of this very civilized city, affected by the charm of its scenery and by the poetic pleasures to be enjoyed on the shores of its renowned West Lake, the Painting Academy was instilled with a new lyricism. The rugged peaks and wind-swept plains of the northern schools of landscape were ill-suited to this gentler mood; the styles of Kuo Hsi and Fan K'uan continued to be practiced by some painters in the north, under the Chin invaders, but only as minor local traditions. The style of Li T'ang proved more adaptable to the tendencies of the relocated Academy, and was followed by most of its landscapists. Successive transformations of this style, moving always in the direction of mildness and intimacy, form the basis of Southern Sung Academy landscape.

A few artists carried on older traditions, some of them working in archaistic styles. An antiquarian taste, which had arisen among scholarly collectors during the late Northern Sung, stimulated the imitation of T'ang and earlier painting. A descendant of the first Sung emperor, Chao Po-chü, adopted the "blue-and-green" manner of the T'ang dynasty landscapists. One of the many paintings attributed to him is the small fan-shaped picture known as *The Han Palace*. It is unsigned, and the attribution unconvincing; the landscape is not painted in the blue-and-green manner at all, and some details, such as the figures, the twisted plum trees and the blue mountains beyond, point to a date in the late twelfth or early thirteenth century, long after the death of the purported artist. The archaic flavor of the composition and the nature of the subject account for the attribution to Chao Po-chü, who specialized in such palace pictures. It is a scene of twilight on the day of the Double Seven, the autumn festival of the legendary Oxherd and Spinning-maid. In the foreground, servants gather with oxen and carts, perhaps for a pageant. The empress and her retinue proceed from the lamplit palace through a natural tunnel in the fantastically eroded rock toward a tower in the upper left. The last light is fading, and they will ascend the tower to engage in the traditional pastime of this evening, gazing at the moon.

The school of Chinese landscape most familiar to the West is the Ma-Hsia school, named after its founders, Ma Yüan and Hsia Kuei. They and their countless followers painted pictures of such broad and immediate appeal that they have, in addition to their great popularity in their homeland, remained the favorites of foreigners through the centuries. Thousands of works by the followers, and a few originals by Ma and Hsia themselves, were carried abroad by travelers and merchants, first to Korea and Japan (where the imitations were imitated in their turn, and became the models for a whole school of landscape) and later to Europe and America, where they created the standard Occidental image of Chinese painting. Most Chinese critics, by contrast, have admired the productions of the Ma-Hsia school only moderately, preferring on the whole the landscapes of the Northern Sung period which preceded, and of the Yüan dynasty which followed, the Southern Sung.

Both Ma Yüan and Hsia Kuei were active at the end of the twelfth century and in the first quarter of the thirteenth; both are classed as followers of Li T'ang, although it is unlikely that they could have studied with him directly, since Li probably died during their childhood, or perhaps even before their births. Very little is recorded about the personal life of either of them. Ma Yüan belonged to a family of painters; his father, grandfather and great-grandfather had all served in the Academy, and the evolution of the style that he brought to maturity may have taken place largely within this family tradition. The typical works connected with him seem remote from Li T'ang, even though the continuing influence of that master is discernible in them. Both the album leaves reproduced here use the diagonally divided composition of the Li T'ang school, and the drawing of the rocks derives ultimately from Li's style. But very much has changed. The subject is brought closer, the field of vision narrowed. In his *Myriad Trees and Strange Peaks* (p. 42), Li T'ang had presented a cool, aloof view of mountains in mist, a segment of a vast and imposing prospect. Nature in the works of Ma Yüan has been tamed and idealized, relieved of all but its most agreeable aspects. The scholar who strolls along a mountain path in one picture, and his counterpart in the other who leans on a rock, gazing meditatively at a pair of deer drinking from the stream, express in their postures a sense of security that the relatively rare humans in Northern Sung landscapes could scarcely have felt, awed as they were by the magnitude and mystery of their surroundings.

The theme of Ma Yüan's signed album leaf titled *Walking on a Mountain Path in Spring* is the same as that of the larger-scale work by his son Ma Lin (p. 64): the conscious enjoyment of nature. A scholar walking with his servant on a path along a stream bank stops momentarily to watch two orioles in the wind-blown willow. A verse couplet is written at the right: "Brushed by his sleeves, wild flowers dance in the wind; fleeing from him, the hidden birds cut short their songs." The picture is a distillation of mood, everything in it subservient to the production of a well-defined effect. Nothing is extraneous, and the profusion of interesting detail found in the work of Kuo Hsi and earlier landscapists is gone. The result of this rigorous elimination of the unessential is not austerity, however, but poetry; like the T'ang lyricists and the Japanese *haiku*

Anonymous, late twelfth century (misleading attribution to Chao Po-chü): The Han Palace.
Album leaf. Ink and colors on silk. (w. 9⅝″) Palace Museum Collection, Taichung.

觸袖野花多自舞
避人幽鳥不成啼

Ma Yüan (fl. c. 1190-1230): Walking on a Mountain Path in Spring. Album leaf.
Ink and light colors on silk. (10¾×17″) Palace Museum Collection, Taichung.

poets, Ma Yüan envelops his subject in an aura of feeling with an extreme economy of means, relying upon the emotional associations of his images and the evocative power of the emptiness surrounding them.

The album leaf owned by Mr. C. C. Wang is unsigned, but is one of a pair, the other of which bears an apparently genuine signature. Ma Yüan here employs his most typical composition, the one which earned him the nickname "One-corner Ma" from his contemporaries. In delicate gradations of ink tone, he opens behind the sharply drawn foreground group a middle distance bounded by the dim silhouettes of leafy trees, and a limitless void beyond that. The gaze of the viewer is inevitably drawn back into this void, moving from the material world to one without substance; and the universal human proneness to associate space with spirituality gives to the experience a touch of the mystical.

Hsia Kuei carries even further the simplification of design and elimination of solid form, scarcely defining the textures of surfaces, obscuring even larger parts of his pictures in mist. Line is reduced to a minimum, and much of that is merely the edges of areas of wash, but this minimum is so telling that it brings the entire composition into focus. Together with the consummately skillful handling of graded washes, in which the Southern Sung painters excelled all others, it establishes firmly the positions of solid elements within the picture space, leaving the viewer with no sense of doubt about its

Ma Yüan (fl. c. 1190-1230): A Scholar and His Servant on a Terrace. Album leaf.
Ink and light colors on silk. (9¾×10¼″) C. C. Wang Collection, New York.

structure, even providing his imagination with clues as to how the extensive empty areas should be filled. In his own way, then, Hsia Kuei adheres to the Academy canons, since he presents clearly whatever he chooses to present at all.

The radical abbreviation of design and form in the small paintings that make up most of Hsia Kuei's surviving output allows one to absorb their content in a single glance, and prolonged study only fills out and deepens the initial impression. His paintings in handscroll form produce the same impression of instantaneous disclosure, even though the viewing of a handscroll necessarily takes place over a period of time. The eye is led in and out, from solid to space and back, each segment existing in itself as a brief, crystalline visual statement. The detail reproduced here, with a massive boulder set against evocative evening mists, is from the scroll titled *A Pure and Remote View of Streams and Mountains*, perhaps the supreme masterpiece of the whole Ma-Hsia school. The fact that it is painted on paper instead of silk allows the brilliance of the brushwork to be appreciated: dry strokes applied with a slanting brush for the rock surface, the foliage done with a split brush (the fibers of the tip divided), the frail bridge and solitary traveler drawn in line that is firm but not stiff. What the Chinese praise most highly, however, is Hsia Kuei's control of ink values, from the subtlest washes to the richest black. This technical prowess is used with discipline and restraint. Critics of later centuries, who often found the works of Ma Yüan and other Southern Sung academicians too sweet for their taste, treated Hsia Kuei more favorably, preferring his cooler approach and (in the somewhat moralistic Chinese view) more chaste expression.

The master of the school who has been most unjustly treated is Ma Lin, son of Ma Yüan. He began his career overshadowed by four generations of famous ancestors; his father, the story goes, was so anxious for Ma Lin to attain an eminent position in the Academy that he sometimes signed "Ma Lin" to his own works, hoping to enhance the son's reputation. It may have done so, but can hardly have helped the younger Ma's self-confidence. Judging from extant works of Ma Lin, he was quite capable of standing alone. In addition to the superb *Listening to the Wind in the Pines* (p. 64), a number of small signed paintings by him may be seen in various collections. One of them, *Waiting for Guests by Lamplight*, belongs among the most exquisite of all Southern Sung creations in the idyllic mode. As twilight falls in a palace courtyard, a nobleman sits at the entrance to a pavilion, preparing to welcome guests to a night banquet. Servants outside stand ready to light candles along the path between flowering trees. Color is used with unusual effectiveness in imparting the feeling of this moment: a yellow moon in a dusky blue-green sky, blue hills, a glow of yellow lamplight under the eaves, pale green leaves and violet blossoms on the trees. The Chinese title of the picture refers to verses by the T'ang poet Li Po, on a theme which must have suited the spirit of the Hang-chou court in these last, declining decades of the dynasty: since life is so brief, it suggests, we must light candles and make the most of the hours of darkness.

Appraisals of Ma Lin by both Chinese and Western writers have generally been based on works as orthodox as this, and have dismissed him as a faded facsimile of Ma Yüan. But some things in his pictures suggest that the real Ma Lin, a more complex

Hsia Kuei (fl. c. 1190-1230): A Pure and Remote View of Rivers and Mountains. Section of a handscroll. Ink on paper. (H. 18¼") Palace Museum Collection, Taichung.

artistic personality than the critics have recognized, has slipped away from them. The degree of tension and unrest, for example, in his *Listening to the Wind in the Pines*, is something hostile to the complacency of Academy landscape, and the preciosity of the figure seems suspiciously deliberate. It is as if the painter had tried in this work to push beyond acceptable limits some features of Ma-Hsia landscape—the refinement of line and wash, the idealization of natural forms, the assertion of man's emotional responsiveness to nature—and so bring to culmination, and to an end, this species of landscape painting. It proved, in any event, no longer viable, and was never again practiced with the same conviction or success.

The future of Chinese painting lay outside the Academy; but the direction it was to take is accurately forecast in another small signed work by Ma Lin, one that reveals him as a still more enigmatic figure. Titled *The Fragrance of Spring: Clearing After Rain*, it is a picture of trees, bamboo and briers growing in disorderly profusion on the banks of a stream. Mists drift over the marshy ground and among the trees. An aged and

Ma Lin (fl. mid-thirteenth century): Waiting for Guests by Lamplight. Album leaf.
Ink and colors on silk. (9¾×9⅞″) Palace Museum Collection, Taichung.

twisted plum tree, growing from between rocks, puts forth new buds; the exuberant regeneration of plants in spring is revealed as an unruly force, and no effort is made to idealize it. On the further shore of the stream, a splintered tree stump stands as just the stark memorial to death and decay that all standard landscapes of the school had diligently excluded. From the pleasure parks of orthodox Ma-Hsia landscape (including most of Ma Lin's own), we are brought back suddenly to the real, unkempt world. Much of the school manner is preserved—the rocks are Ma Yüan's, and the trees are obviously by the same hand that drew those in the *Waiting for Guests by Lamplight*; but it is applied to a composition in which the canons of the Academy are violated, and turned to the excitation of feelings quite outside the fairly narrow range of the Academy taste. The painting thus anticipates developments in the Yüan and later dynasties, when there was no longer to be any fixed relation between a style and the expressive uses to which it was put.

Ma Lin (fl. mid-thirteenth century): The Fragrance of Spring: Clearing After Rain. Album leaf.
Ink and light colors on silk. (10¾×16⅜″) Palace Museum Collection, Taichung.

The Literati and Ch'an Painters of the Sung Dynasty

8

UNTIL the second half of the eleventh century, the theory of painting spoken of in the previous chapters as the traditional one in China, the notion that a painting of a given object or scene should evoke in the person who sees it thoughts and feelings akin to those that the actual object or scene would evoke, was never seriously challenged. By then, however, some scholars concerned with painting had become aware of the inadequacy of this theory to explain the peculiar expressive power of certain unorthodox styles and techniques that had been gaining popularity during the preceding few centuries. Pictures that failed to offer reasonably faithful renderings of natural forms should, according to the traditional belief, fail to produce any very strong response in the viewer, since they obviously could no longer make him "feel as though he were gazing at the thing (or place) itself." But the excitement generated by some of these radical departures from visual truthfulness could not be denied. A new theory was required to account for it.

The theory was formulated by members of a remarkable coterie of scholars which had for its central figure the great poet, prose writer, statesman, calligrapher and painter Su Shih (1036-1101), better known as Su Tung-p'o. He and his friends belonged to the literati class, and accordingly devoted their main energies to administrative service in the bureaucracy, study of the classics, literary composition, and other pursuits considered suitable as the major concerns of men of letters. In their spare time they painted, and argued and wrote about painting. The school they founded became known as *wen-jen hua*, or "literati painting."

The theory of painting held by these scholar-artists reflected their Confucian background. Poetry and music, and later calligraphy, had long been treated in Confucian writings as vehicles for embodying one's personal thought and feeling, for conveying to others something of one's very nature. In calligraphy, this was accomplished through abstract means, the expressiveness of line and form, interest and individuality of brushwork. The new and eccentric styles which grew out of the *i-p'in* or "untrammeled class" of painting made use of these same means, and so opened the way for painting to be recognized as fulfilling a like function. The quality of a painting, said the literati writers, reflects the personal quality of the artist; its expressive content derives from

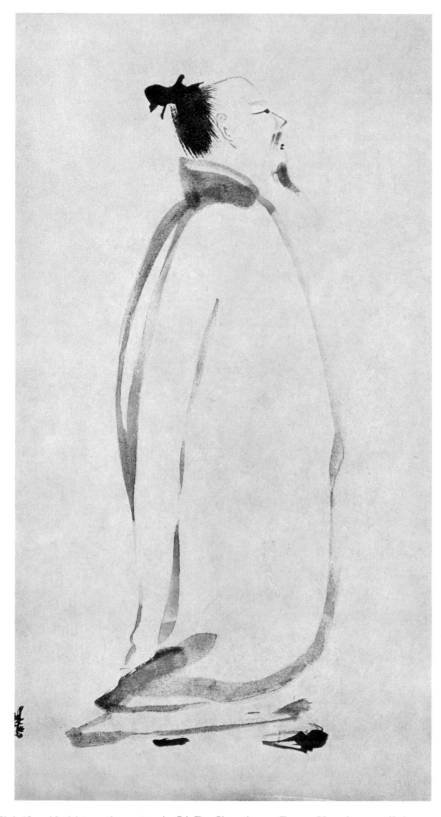

Liang K'ai (fl. mid-thirteenth century): Li Po Chanting a Poem. Hanging scroll (cropped at top). Ink on paper. (w. 12⅛″) Commission for the Protection of Cultural Properties, Tokyo.

his mind, and has no necessary relationship to anything the artist or the viewer thinks or feels about the object represented. The value of the picture does not depend upon its likeness to anything in nature. The object in nature serves as raw material which must be transformed into an artistic idiom, and the mode of this transformation, the character of the lines and forms produced by the brush, reveals something about the person who drew them, and about his mood at the moment he drew them. "Anyone who talks about painting in terms of likeness," writes Su Tung-p'o, "deserves to be classed with the children."

All this seems precocious in relation to Occidental art theory, anticipating ideas which did not appear in the West until well into the nineteenth century. The paintings produced by the literati artists were equally remarkable for their time. They usually worked in ink only, and often used deliberately amateurish-looking techniques. Marked distortions of form appear in their pictures: sometimes in an archaistic spirit, referring by touches of naïveté and awkwardness to the styles of archaic periods, before certain problems of representation had been solved; sometimes according to the whim of the moment, making an impression of pure arbitrariness. They painted for themselves and their friends, giving the pictures as presents, angrily refusing any offers to buy them. The reaction among those outsiders who did not share their taste was much like the initial popular reaction to Post-Impressionism in Europe: "Likeness is what is *valued* in painting!" exclaims an indignant Southern Sung writer, aroused by the lines of Su Tung-p'o just quoted. "Anyone who doesn't catch a likeness might as well not paint at all."

If, nine centuries later, we feel a kinship of ideals with these early literati artists, we are understandably eager to see their provocative paintings; but very few have survived. We must be content, for the most part, with works by their close followers, and even these are scarce. In the absence of any reliable paintings by the leading landscapist of the group, Mi Fu (1052-1109), some clue to the nature of his achievements may be sought in a few extant pictures by his son, Mi Yu-jen. Mi Fu was an antiquarian and collector; familiar with old manners of painting, he incorporated elements from them into his own works. Chinese critics trace the sources of his style to the tenth century master Tung Yüan, and to one of the "ink-splashers" of the T'ang period, Wang Mo. A distant reference to the splashing technique, in which the shapes of landscape elements were partially determined by the chance configurations of freely spattered ink, is probably present in the very wet application of ink and in the somewhat arbitrary appearance of mountains and trees in landscapes by Mi Yu-jen, although these were evidently painted with a brush. The picture in the former Abe collection, Osaka, is the oddest of them all, with its strangely shadowed peaks and drifting mists. Some of the vagueness of outline in it is the fault of damage and retouching, but better-preserved works by Mi Yu-jen have the same diffuse quality, which must have been an essential ingredient of the style. The fairly sparse scattering of *tien*, or dots, is at sharp variance with the standard "Mi style" as employed by imitators of later centuries, in which landscape forms are built up in a pointillist manner with clusters of such dots.

Mi Yu-jen (1086-1165): Mountains in Clouds. Hanging scroll. Ink on paper. (9¾×11½")
Osaka Municipal Museum (former Abe Collection).

Another major literati painter of this age was Li Kung-lin (1040-1106), who remains a somewhat problematic figure in spite of the many excellent works attributed to him. Important in his painting was the element of archaism; he imitated T'ang masters, and his most characteristic manner, the method of drawing in fine ink line known as *pai-miao*, is supposed to have been based on the figure painting of Wu Tao-tzu. Among the finest works of the Li Kung-lin school is a long handscroll attributed to one of his followers, a Ch'an Buddhist monk of the twelfth century named Fan-lung. It is a series of portraits of Arhats, disciples of the historical Buddha who were customarily depicted as aged recluses, and often shown in landscape settings, as is the Arhat in our detail. He stands alone in the forest, leaning against the trunk of a pine, his loose robe billowing in the wind. Two small deer approach, carrying flowers in their mouths as offerings. The curving tree trunks serve here, as in the *Noble Scholar under a Willow* (p. 63), to frame and echo a human mood, but the Arhat himself remains, like the poet in the other picture, introspective. In contrast to the fluid, delicate lineament of the figure, the landscape is built up in strokes of a less fixed character, made at some points with a semi-dry brush to produce a rich, charcoal-like line. Occasionally rough and scratchy, the brushwork manifests a taste quite opposed to that of the Academy, where firm, elegant lineament was standard.

Attributed to Mu-ch'i (fl. mid-thirteenth century): Evening Glow on a Fishing Village, from Eight Views of the Hsiao-Hsiang Region. Section of a handscroll. Ink on paper. (H. 13″) Nezu Art Museum, Tokyo.

Attributed to Fan-lung (twelfth century): An Arhat in the Forest. Section of a handscroll. Ink on paper. (H. 12″)
Freer Gallery of Art, Washington, D.C.

As for the paintings of Su Tung-p'o himself, it is questionable whether any at all have survived. His favorite subjects were bamboo and old trees, and these motives accordingly became popular among his numerous followers. A short handscroll combining the two, painted by a nephew of Mi Fu named Wang T'ing-yün, is the best extant representative of the genre. The trunk and branches of an old, moss-grown tree, a few stalks of bamboo beside it, make up the commonplace subject matter of the picture. Because the import of such paintings depends so largely upon formal qualities bound up with brush, ink and paper, what is represented matters less. A subject that does not assert its own interest or beauty is in fact preferable. As an unidealized rendering of an unexciting theme, the painting might have fallen into the severe intellectuality that sometimes afflicts works of this kind, but is saved by its surface richness. Contrasts of wetness and dryness in the application of ink provide a varied texture, and a diversity of brush techniques are employed: a broken, dragged stroke for the rough bark, mottled patches for the moss, a shaded stroke made with an unevenly-inked brush for twigs, and others.

An inscription by the artist is mounted in the scroll after the painting, and a series of colophons by other writers follow. The reading of such colophons is for the Chinese a part of the experience of seeing the picture, since they reveal how it was enjoyed and evaluated by earlier connoisseurs. One of them on this scroll, by a fourteenth century theorist named T'ang Hou, is especially enlightening, and worthy of translation in part:

> "The scholar-gentleman turns to painting as a form of play. Often the images he paints take on new forms beneath his random brush, and a scene comes forth, exuberant and fresh... Wang T'ing-yün, with the overflow of energy from his activities as *littérateur* and calligrapher, devoted himself to "ink-plays"... This painting of *Secluded Bamboo and a Withered Tree* is simple in substance but antique in conception... What was for him only a means of giving lodging to a moment's exhilaration is passed down over a hundred generations, and all who see its torn silk and remnant paper must gaze in admiration, loving and revering it. He may truly be called a man of accomplishment. (Signed:) T'ang Hou, whose hand cannot forbear going on to add his encomium:
>
>> "Set forth your heart, without reserve,
>>   And your brush will be inspired.
>> Writing and painting serve a single aim,
>>   The revelation of innate goodness.
>> Here are two companions,
>>   An old tree and tall bamboo,
>> Metamorphosed by his unreined hand,
>>   Finished in an instant.
>> The embodiment of a single moment
>>   Is the treasure of a hundred ages,
>> And one feels, unrolling it, a fondness,
>>   As if seeing the man himself."

This, the theorists maintain, is the proper response to a painting by one of the scholar artists: one does not feel "as if he were in the very place," or "as if seeing the thing itself"; but as if one had come face to face with the man. The mind of the artist, and not the bamboo or landscape, is the real subject of the picture.

Associated with the Su Tung-p'o circle were several Ch'an Buddhist monks who were also amateur painters. Nothing remains from their hands, nor have the works of Ch'an painters in the following generations survived in any number—the scroll attributed to Fan-lung is an isolated example. Numerous paintings by their artistic descendants of the late Sung and early Yüan dynasties are preserved in Japan, however, having been brought there along with the Ch'an doctrine. The Ch'an school of painting in the thirteenth century was centered in monasteries located in the hills around Hang-chou, and especially in one of them, the Liu-t'ung-ssu. The abbot of this monastery was Mu-ch'i, a pupil of the Ch'an master Wu-chun who is portrayed in the Tōfukuji portrait (p. 48), and the greatest of the Ch'an artists. The Chinese have never given Mu-ch'i the attention and respect he deserves. Almost all the extant works by him or attributed to him are in Japan, where he has, by contrast, been recognized as one of the greatest masters of any period.

Although the number of paintings attributed to him in Japan is quite large, in only a few cases is there any firm basis for the attribution. Among the more problematic

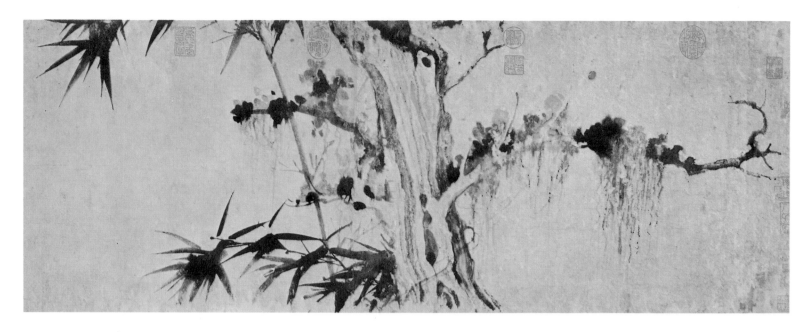

Wang T'ing-yün (1151-1202): Secluded Bamboo and Withered Tree. Section of a handscroll. Ink on paper. (H. 15″)
Fujii Yūrinkan, Kyoto.

works, the landscapes in the series *Eight Views of the Hsiao-Hsiang Region* rank high in quality, and appear to be at least of the period and school of Mu-ch'i. In their wet brushwork and dissolution of form, they follow the stylistic tradition of Mi Yu-jen; the affinities between one of them, *Evening Glow on a Fishing Village*, and the small Mi Yu-jen picture reproduced on the opposite page are especially obvious. The Ch'an artist conveys a stronger sense of swiftness and vigor, working chiefly in simple washes and broad, scratchy strokes made with a straw brush. Drawing in line is reduced to minimal indications: trunks of trees, roofs of houses, a few fishermen in boats. It is the wonder of the painting that a convincing impression of light and shade, mist and space, is created with these simple means. There is none of that sense of withdrawal from nature that one feels in the Mi Yu-jen landscape. The expressionist demands of the amateur school of painting are reconciled with the traditional Chinese view; the painting is not only moving in purely ink-on-paper terms, but also functions as an image— abbreviated, impressionistic, but nonetheless compelling—of the external world.

The same statement can be applied to the Wang T'ing-yün painting, so that no general distinction between the literati and Ch'an schools is intended by it. It may be questioned whether a valid division can in fact be made, whether they should not be regarded as a single school of amateur artists. In styles they overlap; perhaps they should be distinguished, if at all, on the basis of attitude: the more intellectual approach of the Confucian literatus as against the intuitive one of the Ch'an monk. The Ch'an painter's awareness of a single reality underlying the seemingly disjunct phenomena of nature is communicated with the same immediacy as the truths of the Ch'an doctrine, which cannot be conveyed by translating them into the intellectual concepts of ordinary

Mu-ch'i (fl. mid-thirteenth century): Mother Monkey and Child. Detail from a hanging scroll. Ink on silk. Daitokuji, Kyoto.

discourse and expecting the listener to translate them back into something like the original impulse. The Ch'an artist typically defines his subject only at a few key points, leaving the rest ambiguous, suggestive rather than descriptive. The viewer completes the image, as the Ch'an novice pieces out by intuition the cryptic utterances of the master.

The masterpieces of Mu-ch'i, and the works that can be most confidently ascribed to him, are the three paintings now kept as a triptych in the Daitokuji, the great Zen Buddhist temple in Kyoto. These are no spontaneous "ink-plays," but works profoundly conceived. The two side pieces, representing a crane and monkeys, were probably complete as a pair originally, with the central figure of Kuan-yin a separate picture. The combination into a triptych was a fortunate one, however; the three are in perfect accord, and seem to signify a like accord between two realms of being usually considered remote from each other, below and above humankind, the animal and the divine. Kuan-yin, represented as a white-robed woman, sits in meditation with downcast eyes, while the monkey mother, clasping her child, gazes into the eyes of the observer with the disconcerting directness of a Ch'an parable. The branch on which the monkeys rest is painted in loose, rough strokes of dilute ink, similar to those used in the Wang T'ing-yün picture, with no more trace of obvious skill in the technique than there is of outward beauty in the subject.

The Liu-t'ung-ssu, in this same period, was the haven for a fugitive from the Imperial Academy named Liang K'ai. He was not forced by failure to quit the academy; he had, in fact, been awarded the highest honor for painters-in-attendance, the Golden Girdle. He left this insigne of rank hanging on the wall, the story goes, and departed—whether for reasons of artistic dissatisfaction or a non-conformist temperament, we cannot say. Liang K'ai's teacher was a follower of Li Kung-lin, and Liang himself is supposed to have used that master's *pai-miao* technique in his early works. Later he developed his famous "abbreviated brushwork" manner of figure painting. His pictures in this freer manner presumably belong to the period of his association with Mu-ch'i and other Ch'an artists, although, since the rough and abbreviated styles were not by any means used exclusively by the Ch'an Buddhists, he may well have arrived at it independently.

The poet Li Po, in Liang K'ai's imaginary portrait, walks with head raised, chanting a poem. With deceptively simple drawing, limited to a dozen or so strokes for the head and about as many more for the robe and feet, the exhilaration of the poet is deftly caught. The long lines of the robe belong to the non-descriptive brushwork of the amateur styles; their air of freedom and relaxation has nothing to do with the fabric they outline, but rather contributes to the whole aspect of the figure, outwardly calm but charged with an inner vitality. Like Mu-ch'i, Liang K'ai answers two difficult-to-reconcile sets of criteria: those of the Academy, which required that the subject be convincingly portrayed and adequately characterized, and those of the amateur painters, who believed that the significance of the picture is inseparable from its formal properties, and that the brushstrokes which compose it must be independently meaningful.

The Early Yüan Painters
Ch'ien Hsüan, Chao Meng-fu, Kao K'o-kung

9

At the end of the twelfth century the Sung state, now confined to the area below the Yangtze River, had achieved an uneasy kind of peace with its northern neighbors, the Chin Tartars. By the beginning of the thirteenth, however, a more formidable threat had appeared in the north. The Mongols, led first by the great Jenghiz Khan and later by his son Ogodai and grandson Khubilai, had begun that campaign of conquest which was to win for them the largest empire in the history of the world. The Chin were destroyed by 1234; Hang-chou fell in 1276, and the Sung dynasty came to an end three years later. The dynasty set up by the Mongols to rule the whole of China, with Khubilai Khan as emperor and a capital on the present site of Peking, was given the name Yüan.

During the perilous years of transition, many of the Confucian literati, who would ordinarily have held positions in the central government or local administrations, went into cautious retirement. Even after peace was restored, a great number of them declined, out of loyalty to the fallen Sung or for more practical reasons, to emerge from seclusion and accept office under the foreign rulers. A kind of scholarly sub-society of "recluses" came into being, centered in the small area between the old capital, Hang-chou, and the Yangtze River. There, in small local coteries, they devoted themselves to the favorite scholarly activities: visiting one another, writing poems, practicing calligraphy and painting. It was among these scholars that the school of literati painting, more or less dormant since the early Southern Sung, began to be revived.

The early Yüan painters inherited no such healthy traditions as had those of the early Sung. The Imperial Academy was defunct, and its styles virtually so. Ch'an Buddhist painters, although still active, were too scattered and independent to form a school, and no artists of major rank had succeeded Liang K'ai and Mu-ch'i. The literati painters rejected both: the styles of the Academy as too overtly appealing (compare the rejection of romantic values in the late nineteenth and twentieth century West), and Ch'an painting because, in their view, it lacked discipline and had carried the rough manners of brushwork to excess. Two courses were open to them, those always open to artists dissatisfied with the present and the immediate past: archaism and innovation, the revival of old styles and the creation of new ones. Like their late Northern Sung predecessors, the literati painters of the early Yüan chose to combine the two.

Ch'ien Hsüan (c. 1235-1301), probably copy after Han Kan (eighth century): Yang Kuei-fei Mounting a Horse. Section of a handscroll. Ink and colors on paper. (H. 11⅝") Freer Gallery of Art, Washington, D.C.

The movement began in Wu-hsing, north of Hang-chou; the foremost participants were Ch'ien Hsüan and his pupil Chao Meng-fu. Ch'ien was one of those who had gone into retirement and refused to serve the Mongols. When Chao, about twenty years younger and still at the threshold of his career, traveled to Peking in 1286 to become a minister at the court of Khubilai Khan, Ch'ien remained behind and spent his time in painting, composing poetry and drinking. He painted figures, birds and flowers, and landscapes, nearly always with some stylistic reference to pre-Southern Sung painting. His figure compositions were mostly based on T'ang dynasty models, with intervening influence from the originator of this archaistic mode, Li Kung-lin. In them, a style that had once breathed warm life and human emotion takes on, through the passage of centuries and the veneration of connoisseurs, a cool and classicistic air. The short handscroll representing *Yang Kuei-fei Mounting a Horse* is a good example. It may have been copied from a composition by the eighth century horse painter Han Kan; but Han, a court painter for Ming-huang himself, would surely have portrayed this subject—which combines the emperor's two greatest loves, beautiful women and fine horses—with more warmth than Ch'ien Hsüan displays.

This very coolness is the essence of Chien Hsüan's painting: unimpassioned, fastidious, sensitive, seldom immediately appealing. In his landscapes he revived the blue-and-green manner, following Chao Po-chü, who had himself employed it as an archaistic manner derived from the T'ang dynasty masters. Art based on art based on art: with every level of stylistic reference the work withdraws further from the original impulse, the direct experience of nature, and begins to demand in both the artist and his audience a higher degree of aesthetic sophistication, an acquaintance and concern with the history of style. The archaism of the literati painters was not so much a matter of wholehearted, admiring imitation of early painting as of stylistic allusion, the calculated evocation of the past with all its associations. We are familiar with such evocative allusion today: Stravinsky playing upon Tchaikowsky or the Baroque, T.S. Eliot shifting into a Spenserian language, Picasso referring to primitive or Hellenic styles.

For his paintings in the antique blue-and-green manner, Ch'ien Hsüan chose suitably antique themes. One of them represents Wang Hsi-chih, the supreme master of the "grass" or cursive script, gazing at swimming geese from a lakeside pavilion, finding in their sinuous necks a gracefulness of line worthy of imitation in his calligraphy. The very theme is in accord with the literati painters' beliefs: nature supplies form to the artist, but he accepts it as form only, and feels free to utilize it for his private ends. The drawing of rocks and trees, the decorative use of heavy color, the flatness of the design, refer to T'ang painting; but they also, along with a childlike quality in the whole picture, show us Ch'ien Hsüan the primitive, a more delicate and sophisticated Chinese cousin of Henri Rousseau, without that painter's exuberance.

In at least one other of his landscapes, Ch'ien Hsüan attempted a revival and reinterpretation of another early manner, that of the tenth century master Tung Yüan. The attempt was abortive; the painting is more odd than accomplished, too plainly experimental. A more successful essay in the same direction was made by his pupil Chao Meng-fu in the famous *Autumn Colors on the Ch'iao and Hua Mountains*, dated 1295. Chao claimed to have "tried to rid himself absolutely of the styles of the Sung painters," and boasted that his painting, "although it may look simple and rough, will be recognized by the perceptive viewer as being close to the ancients, and therefore truly excellent." His obvious allusions to the Tung Yüan manner include the wavy ground lines, the miniature figures and the "level distance" compositional plan. The picture relates to Tung Yüan in a more subtle way as well: the commonplace quality of the scenery, a marshy plain from which Mt. Ch'iao rises as a breadloaf-like hill. Throughout the picture Chao exhibits a primitivist disregard for correct size relationships, and a rejection of outward beauty; even willows, which in paintings of the Ma Yüan school had assumed an unearthly loveliness, are here devoid of charm. Chao Meng-fu carries the denial of romanticism beyond Ch'ien Hsüan's cool withdrawal, into an austerity of mood that verges on bleakness. The achievements of the Sung dynasty are consciously sacrificed: the graded washes are gone, there is little sense of space and no atmosphere. Since the blank area above the horizon serves no important function in the composition, the painter uses it to write a long inscription, describing the circumstances under which

Ch'ien Hsüan (c. 1235-1301): Wang Hsi-chih Gazing at Geese. Section of a handscroll.
Ink and colors on paper. (H. 9⅛") C. C. Wang Collection, New York.

the picture was painted. Later owners have added an abundance of seals and inscriptions that would have seemed a defacement on a typical Southern Sung landscape, but is quite in keeping with the "literary" character of this one.

Among the high officials who were associates of Chao Meng-fu in the Peking administration was another amateur painter, Kao K'o-kung, who held the position of

President of the Board of Justice. The oldest of the major Yüan landscapists, he was revered by all his younger contemporaries. His extant works are very few, most of them preserved in the Palace Museum Collection. A short handscroll in the same collection titled *Green Hills and White Clouds*, although unsigned and labelled simply as the work of an "Unknown artist of the Yüan period," can be added to this small number on the basis of its style. Like the landscapes of Ch'ien Hsüan and Chao Meng-fu, it is the product of an attempt to create, out of a mixture of old styles and sheer originality, something which satisfied both the archaist taste and the expressive needs of the present. Misty

Chao Meng-fu (1254-1322): Autumn Colors on the Ch'iao and Hua Mountains. Dated 1295. Section of a handscroll. Ink and colors on paper. (H. 11⅛″) Palace Museum Collection, Taichung.

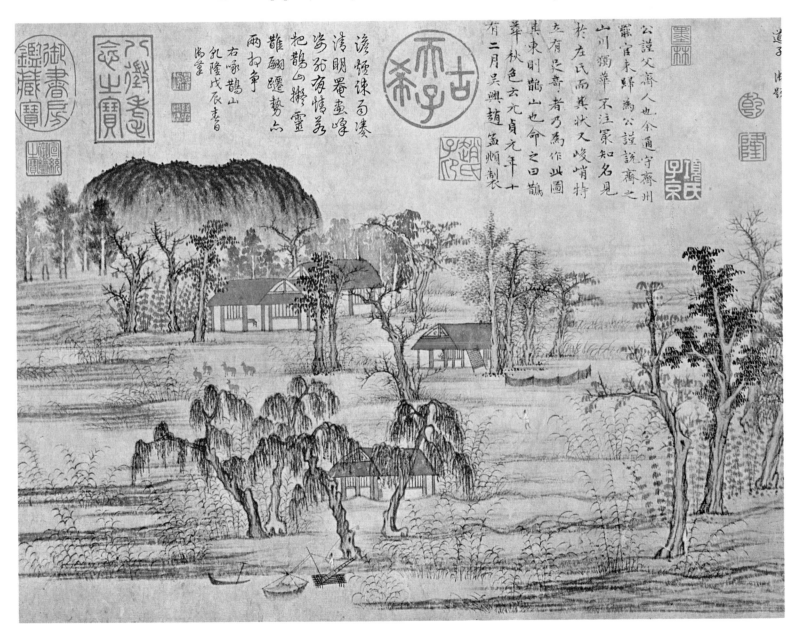

Probably by Kao K'o-kung (1248-1310): Green Hills and White Clouds. Section of a handscroll.
Ink and colors on silk. (H. 19¼″) Palace Museum Collection, Taichung.

groves of trees, naïvely drawn cottages and river banks are adopted closely from the works of a late Northern Sung painter, Chao Ling-jang, while the drawing of the hills and of the archaic hard-edged clouds drifting among them refers more distantly to the styles of Tung Yüan and Mi Fu, whom Kao is said to have imitated. But the impact of the painting depends upon a wholly new use of these old materials. The symmetry of the range of hills, quite contrary to all canons of Sung painting, the strangely disturbing repetition of forms and almost oppressive corporeality of the terrain, are expressionist devices of the artist's own, answering some inner impulse. Chinese theorists write of "mountains within the mind," conceived mysteriously in the painter's unconscious to be externalized on paper or silk in a creative act "without volition." These are surely such mountains of the mind.

Ch'ien Hsüan, Chao Meng-fu and Kao K'o-kung, with some of their contemporaries, inaugurated a new era in Chinese painting. In order to accomplish this, they undertook a revolution of style that was in part destructive, involving the casting-off of outworn and uncongenial modes that sometimes must attend epochs. Many of the achievements of the previous two centuries they willingly sacrificed; their bonds with the past stretched further back, to the Northern Sung and beyond. Their innovations were brilliant but tentative, and did not prove to be final solutions to the problems facing the literati painters of the Yüan period: how to capture, within the limits of the amateur styles, that pictorial coherence and look of "rightness" which they admired in Five Dynasties and early Sung painting; how to give strength and a sense of sureness to their techniques while avoiding an impression of professional finish; how to give freshness and interest to depictions of commonplace subject matter. It was left for the artists of the latter half of the dynasty, the so-called Four Great Masters and their friends and followers, to bring the school of literati painting to full maturity.

The Late Yüan Painters
The Four Great Masters and Sheng Mou

10

AFTER the death of Khubilai Khan, the effectiveness of the Mongol rule in China deteriorated sharply. The reign of the last Mongol emperor, who succeeded to the throne as a boy in 1333, was an era of ever-worsening turbulence, as famines, inflation and the inevitable revolts demoralized all classes of society. More than ever, educated men withdrew from official service and public life to remain in semi-obscurity, awaiting the re-establishment of peaceful conditions.

One of these, and more of a genuine recluse than most, was Wu Chen. Poor by birth and unsociable by nature, he made his living first as a diviner, and later, when his reputation as a painter had spread, by presenting his pictures to friends and receiving gifts in return—a practice unobjectionable to the literati artist, who refused only to work on commission and to subordinate his own taste to that of a patron. Wu Chen painted bamboo and landscapes, usually inscribing on them poems of his own composition. The scenery of his landscapes is that of his home, the moist terrain of the Chiang-nan region, with its network of rivers and canals, its flatness broken only by modest hills. His style, like his subjects, is unassuming, a relaxed manner in which occasional quirks and touches of mild eccentricity appear as small pleasantries.

His best-known work is the *Fishermen* handscroll, a set of variations on a simple theme: the angler in his boat. The "fishermen" are no relatives of those in the Chao Kan scroll, for whom fishing is a livelihood; they are amateur anglers, scholars enjoying their leisure. They sleep, admire the scenery, sing boating songs, but seldom fish. One of them, in the central section of the scroll, sits absorbed in contemplation of three hills of roughly conical shape, their slopes slightly concave. Behind, ranks of similar hillocks rise and fall like waves on the ocean. The repetition of simple forms has something in common with that in the Kao K'o-kung landscape (p. 104), where, however, it is a bit unsettling in effect; here it rather lulls the consciousness. Nevertheless, there is a curious fascination in this orderly arrangement of the terrain, a variety-in-sameness which the Chinese prize. The viewer finds his gaze, along with that of the solitary boatman, arrested by it.

Despite the quiet amiableness of his style, Wu Chen was not a popular painter during his lifetime. In a well-known (and probably apocryphal) anecdote, his wife complained that while crowds of people were visiting another artist who lived nearby,

Wu Chen (1280-1354): Fishermen. Painted in 1342. Section of a handscroll. Ink on paper. (H. 12³/₁₆″)
Freer Gallery of Art, Washington, D.C.

Sheng Mou, bringing gifts to exchange for his pictures, there was little demand for her husband's works. Wu Chen replied that in twenty years it would be otherwise, and so it was: his own reputation rose, and Sheng's declined. Sheng Mou was less the scholar, more the professional painter. Although a follower of Chao Meng-fu, he preserved elements of the technique, along with the warmer mood, of Southern Sung landscape. His handscroll titled *Boating on the River in Autumn* illustrates the ambivalence of his style: the boats, drawn up side by side while their occupants converse, are drawn in delicate line with washes of color, while the river bank and trees are brilliantly painted in freer brushwork. But even this broader manner of Sheng Mou differs markedly from the painting of Wu Chen; and the points of difference, however we ourselves may assess them qualitatively, provide some insight into Chinese criteria of judgement, since it is just these that place Wu Chen far above Sheng Mou in the evaluations of the critics. They maintain that Sheng's relatively tight and crotchety drawing betrays a temperament deficient in the virtues of balance and repose. Wu Chen's looser style, less obviously accomplished, is in the end more admirable. It is characterized by one fourteenth century writer as "profound and remote, with a leisurely and relaxed feeling."

The Yüan master who was to have the most far-reaching effect on later landscape painting, however, was Huang Kung-wang. Chinese writers are unanimous in their enthusiastic acclaim for him. The reasons for this acclaim may not be immediately apparent in his pictures, which are likely to seem unimpressive on first acquaintance. Like Wu Chen, he was content with everyday scenery. Most Northern Sung landscapists had felt obliged to make the individual elements of their picture interesting in themselves; the Southern Sung landscapists, to make them attractive. The literati painters of the Yüan period felt neither compulsion. An outward "plainness," both in subject and style, they regarded as a virtue, and their aim was to produce within this plainness something moving, subtly exciting, personal—"flavor within blandness," as Wu Chen puts it. No painter achieves this better than Huang Kung-wang. Cool and reserved, his paintings represent for the Chinese the perfect expression of an ideal scholarly temperament.

In his technique he continues and advances a mode of painting begun by Sung literati artists, one that departs in important ways from orthodox landscape styles. The artist working in the orthodox styles, using firm, continuous line and clear washes

Sheng Mou (fl. c. 1310-1361): Boating on the River in Autumn. Inscription by a friend of the artist, dated 1361. Section of a handscroll. Ink and colors on paper. (H. 9¾") Palace Museum Collection, Taichung.

Huang Kung-wang (1269-1354): Dwelling in the Fu-ch'un Mountains. Dated 1350. Section of a handscroll.
Ink on paper. (H. 13″) Palace Museum Collection, Taichung.

Ni Tsan (1301-1374): Trees in a River Valley at Yü-shan. Dated 1371. Hanging scroll. Ink on paper. (37½×14⅛″) ▶
C. C. Wang Collection, New York.

of ink or color, was required to plan his design lucidly before beginning to paint, and
to execute it without a trace of hesitancy; alterations and afterthoughts could not be
tolerated. Huang Kung-wang, by contrast, builds his picture through an additive process,

beginning with drawing in dilute ink and working toward darker and drier brushwork, going over the surface repeatedly to slightly alter a shape, to strengthen a contour, to add more texture strokes on the hillsides or more trees on the shore. The line, built up in a like way with richer, drier strokes traced loosely over a pale, wet underdrawing, attains at last the quality sought by the literati painters: strength and character without any apparent display of skill.

Huang Kung-wang's *magnum opus* is the long handscroll titled *Dwelling in the Fu-ch'un Mountains*, a work of his old age. It has been one of the most influential paintings in China, copied and imitated by countless artists. Like Wu Chen's scroll, it portrays the landscape that the artist knew best, in this case the region of the Fu-ch'un mountains, west of Hang-chou. The "mountains" appear as earthy, unimposing hills, with houses in the valleys between them and pavilions on the shore. A slight restlessness is imparted by the wavering line used for the trunks and branches of bare trees and for the sandy shoals that extend into the water. Groves of leafy trees are placed here and there as dark accents, and pointed *tien*, or dots, applied to the hilltops, all with a wonderful informality. Nothing in the picture seems stereotyped or consciously arranged. Huang's own inscription on it contains an enlightening account of how such a picture was executed. He laid out the entire design in one burst of creation, working in an exhilarated state, unconscious of fatigue. He added to it occasionally, when his mood was right. More than three years had passed by the time he decided it was finished. The somewhat arbitrary nature of that decision is suggested by the nature of the picture; it has nothing of the air of inevitability, of an absolute consummation, that the typical Southern Sung landscape conveys. It seems rather to be the product of a series of decisions, some of them a bit capricious, made by the painter at successive stages in the painting process, reflecting his state of mind at the moments when he made them. And yet, and paradoxically perhaps, it achieves the sense of "rightness" or inherent order which the Chinese call *li*, and which Huang Kung-wang in his treatise on landscapes designates as the ultimate desideratum of painting.

A young friend of Huang Kung-wang, Ni Tsan, is accorded by most Chinese writers a rank almost equal to that of Huang himself, although he was a painter of much narrower scope. His father and grandfather had been successful merchants, but his own interests were scholarly and aesthetic. In his youth he used the family wealth to surround himself with rare books, antiquities, calligraphy and paintings. Some time before the outbreak of the rebellions in the last years of the dynasty, he dispersed his property among relatives and friends, and took to a life of wandering. His motives were practical, as it proved; through this renunciation he exempted himself from the pillage that was suffered by other rich landowners, and enjoyed a relatively tranquil old age. He moved about the lakes and rivers of the region by boat, staying sometimes with friends, but always a lonely figure. Something of his desire for escape from human society—unless it be the society of persons carefully selected by himself as "free from vulgarity"—and of his almost morbid passion for cleanliness (he was forever washing himself), lies behind the cool and chaste quality of his landscapes. No people are to be only breaks in a dense wall of interpenetrating masses are narrow clefts out of which streams flow, shallow pockets enclosing clumps of trees and a few buildings, and a single small opening high at the right, through which one glimpses distant waves and so realizes that the horizon is meant to be still higher. This is neither the grand vista of Northern Sung landscape nor the circumscribed view of Southern Sung; there is no stabilizing point of focus, and the boundaries of the picture can scarcely contain the forces generated within it. Patches of brilliant red, orange and green color are spotted about the surface, adding to the powerful unrest as effectively as the absence of color contributes to the sense of quiet in the ink-monochrome paintings of Ni Tsan. It is strange to discover, when one examines the picture in its details, that trees, houses and figures are drawn with the same childlike simplicity and charm as they are in the more restrained of Wang Meng's works.

The Early Ming "Academy" and the Che School
Pien Wen-chin, Tai Chin, Wu Wei

11

THE small area of China within which all of the Four Great Masters and most other important painters of their age lived and worked, the Chiang-nan area south of the Yangtze River, had preserved throughout the Yüan period a degree of aloofness from Mongol control, and sporadic individual displays of anti-Mongol feeling had continued there since the early years of the dynasty, when nationalists stubbornly loyal to the overthrown Sung had favored it as a place of retirement. It was appropriate, then, that the most successful of the many revolts occurring in the late Yüan period, the one which was to place a Chinese ruler again upon the imperial throne, should arise in this region. Chu Yüan-chang, a former Buddhist monk, proclaimed himself prince of an independent Chiang-nan state in 1364; four years later, when his armies succeeded in driving the Mongols from Peking, he ascended the throne as emperor of all China. To the new dynasty he gave the name Ming.

Perhaps as part of a broad effort to restore to the imperial court some traditional Chinese institutions that had been neglected since the Sung period, the early Ming emperors revived the practice of summoning leading painters, conferring official titles upon them and commissioning pictures for their imperial enjoyment and for the decoration of palace buildings. These court painters are sometimes referred to collectively as the "Ming Academy," although there was no organized body of artists, such as had existed in Sung times, which can properly be designated by that term. Several of the emperors were amateur painters; Hsüan-tsung (reigned 1427-1435) in particular produced charming pictures of birds, flowers and animals in a very orthodox style. In this and also as a patron of art, imposing his taste upon the painters under him, he no doubt fancied himself a latter-day Hui-tsung; but neither he nor the artists he patronized and encouraged were capable of matching the achievements of the great Sung emperor and his Academy.

The virtues and the weaknesses of Ming court painting are well illustrated by the work of Pien Wen-chin, who served two emperors in the early fifteenth century. His *Three Friends and Hundred Birds* belongs to a special category of pictures executed for the New Year's celebrations. The "three friends of the cold" are the pine and bamboo, which remain green through the winter, and the flowering plum, which often blossoms before the last snow has melted, while most other plants still lie dormant. These three, in Pien Wen-chin's composition, provide perches for a lively and colorful cluster of birds of many species, a gathering never to be seen in nature, but quite in keeping with the symbolic and decorative intent of the picture. The artist obviously worked in emulation of the great eleventh and twelfth century masters, but succeeds only partially in recapturing the refinement of their drawing, while their deep sympathy for their subjects and orderly pictorial construction escape him entirely. The painting by its very nature

Tai Chin (fl. early fifteenth century): Fishermen on the River. Detail from a handscroll.
Ink and colors on paper. (H. 18⅛") Freer Gallery of Art, Washington, D.C.

Wu Wei (1459-1508): The Pleasures of the Fishing Village. Section of a handscroll.
Ink and colors on paper. (H. 10¾″) Private Collection, Washington, D.C.

invites comparison with, for example, the *Birds in a Thicket of Bamboo and Plum* of
Hui-tsung's time (p. 69), and inevitably suffers from the comparison. Still, it is an
attractive picture, and on as high a level of quality as the Ming dynasty was to reach
in this category of painting.

To work in styles that have lost their vitality, taking as models pictures he feels
to have reached, within those styles, a now-unattainable perfection, is often enough
the unhappy lot of the academician; it was aggravated, in the case of the Ming court
painters, by the disdain in which they and their conservative styles were held by members
of the scholar class. As professional painters, they were confined to a fairly low social
position, and found themselves condemned by the literati for the very conformity to
antique ideals which the demands of their imperial patrons forced upon them. Perhaps
it was the need to escape from this intolerable situation, as much as the palace intrigues
usually mentioned as a cause, which led Tai Chin, one of the most brilliant painters of

Pien Wen-chin (fl. early fifteenth century): The Three Friends and Hundred Birds. Dated 1413.
Detail from a hanging scroll. Ink and colors on silk. Palace Museum Collection, Taichung.

the dynasty, to cut short his career at court after a few years of service under Hsüang-tsung. He returned to his birthplace near Hang-chou, where he attempted to earn his living as a painter. He did not make a success of it, however, and died in poverty. Later, when his own eminence had been recognized and the repetition of his styles by a host of followers had reflected fame back upon him, he came to be regarded as founder of an important school of landscape, called the Che School after his native province of Chekiang.

The tradition of Ma Yüan and Hsia Kuei had persisted in Chekiang as a local school of minor significance since the Southern Sung period, and it was that tradition which Tai Chin revitalized.

His surviving works range in style from careful and thoroughly derivative pieces, done in frank imitation of Ma Yüan, to others in a much freer mode. A hanging scroll in the Palace Museum, titled *Returning Late from a Spring Outing*, belongs (if the attribution to Tai Chin is to be trusted) to his conservative manner, and probably typifies the highly finished compositions that he offered to the emperor during his days at court. The suave assurance of the brushwork, the charm of the subject, must have pleased the taste that commanded into existence the early Ming blue-and-white porcelains and carved lacquers. The use of delicate graded washes to wrap the middle ground in evening mist is worthy of Ma Yüan himself; but above this a prominent ridge, surmounted by a thick growth of trees, fills the space that would, in a typical Southern Sung picture, be given to undefined and evocative distance. The Ming painter, under looser aesthetic discipline, succumbs to the temptation to elaborate, and scatters a profusion of narrative detail about his picture: the returning wanderer knocks at his gate, a servant hurries with a lamp to open it, farmers trudge homeward, a woman drives geese along the river bank, a Buddhist temple and a pavilion appear beyond.

The vigorous and unacademic manner of Tai Chin, as displayed in the signed handscroll *Fishermen on the River*, may be a development of his later years, or may simply reveal the artist released from constraint, painting as he pleases. For this manner, he is less indebted to the Southern Sung academy than to Wu Chen; the cartoon-like drawing of boats and their occupants in thick line recalls the boatmen in Wu's *Fishermen* scroll (p. 108). But there is more of nervousness in the swift, scratchy treatment of trees, reeds, rocks and marshy shoals than the quiet taste of the Yüan dynasty literati painter would have tolerated. With well-justified pride in the brilliance of his technique, Tai Chin gives a virtuoso performance in descriptive drawing, catching postures and gestures, laying out tangled reeds and mud flats with a dazzling spontaneity.

Tai Chin's leading follower was Wu Wei, who, despite a non-conformist temperament and an unwillingness to heed criticism, served successfully under two Ming emperors. His fondness for alcohol (he is reported to have come into the imperial presence drunk on occasion), in combination with the wildness of his painting style, place him in that long lineage which extends from the drunken ink-splashers of the late T'ang to Hsü Wei and Chu Ta in the late Ming and Ch'ing dynasties. Like Tai Chin, he worked in several markedly different manners. Most common are his large, showy landscapes with figures, painted in ink on silk. Another manner, which follows closely the style of the Tai Chin handscroll, is to be seen in *The Pleasures of the Fishing Village*. The brush line is more rough and impulsive than Tai Chin's, and the drawing, evidently done with a worn, stubby brush, is more carefree. The impressionist treatment of the setting, given a special depth and brilliance by the addition of light brown and blue tones to the splotchy washes of ink, illustrates the statement of a critic that Wu Wei "splashed his ink like scattered clouds."

The fishermen themselves are depicted with an earthy humor that was thought suitable, in Chinese as in much European genre painting, to representations of common-life subjects; the deep sympathy for the hardships undergone by fishermen in reality, set forth so movingly in the greatest of fishermen scrolls, that attributed to Chao Kan, is lost in later centuries. They cluster in boats drawn up among drying nets, chatting companionably and drinking wine. Their naked children play beside them, their wives busy themselves with cooking. A leisurely scholar, escaping the heat of summer in a riverside cottage, leans from his upstairs window to regard the scene.

The drawing of the boats and boatmen again recalls Wu Chen, but if one tries to transplant them in imagination to a Wu Chen picture, he realizes that these gregarious, gesticulating figures would find no comfortable place there. They need the bravura of Wu Wei's landscape style to set off their own animation. As happens so often when the professional artist borrows stylistic features from the amateur (or vice versa) and the distinction between them seems about to dissolve, differences in mood and approach prove in the end more significant than the similarities.

The Che School remained an active force in Ming painting into the sixteenth century, but then declined, as its adherents drifted in one or the other of two directions. Many second-rate artists, anxious to make their works appear more exciting than they really were, carried to uncouth excess the tendencies toward nervousness, over-intensity and mannerism that were inherent already in some works of Tai Chin himself. These are the men chiefly responsible for the bitter condemnation that the school was to incur from late Ming critics, who exempt only Tai Chin, and occasionally Wu Wei, from their scornful comments. A smaller number of painters of greater sensitivity and ability cultivated the less showy styles of the scholar-amateurs, adopting so much from them as to be all but absorbed into the literati school. Thus, having lost its viability and to a large degree even its identity, this movement, which takes its place in retrospect as a kind of epilogue to Southern Sung academy painting, came to an end.

◄   Attributed to Tai Chin (fl. early fifteenth century): Returning Late from a Spring Outing. Hanging scroll. Ink and light colors on silk. (66×32¾") Palace Museum Collection, Taichung.

The Wu School
Shen Chou, Wen Cheng-ming and their Followers

12

THE first century of the Ming dynasty passed without bringing any notable new developments in the literati school of painting. The generation following the Four Great Masters of the late Yüan produced some capable artists, but for the most part they were content to imitate and synthesize the individual achievements of their predecessors. The activity of the school remained localized in the Chiang-nan region, and especially in the vicinity of Su-chou, which had become a major center of the scholarly culture. The group of painters who finally, in the late fifteenth and early sixteenth centuries, re-established the literati tradition as the leading force in Chinese painting, lived in Wu-hsien, the area around Su-chou, and were known accordingly as the Wu School. Most of them belonged to gentry families, received solid Confucian educations and partook of the feeling of security and well-being that permeated urban society in the middle Ming period. Few of them exhibited anything like the anti-social bent of so many Yüan painters, or the violent non-conformism of the late Ming and early Ch'ing individualists. The dominant tone of their paintings, one of sanity and balance, was set by the founder of the school, Shen Chou.

Born into one of the most distinguished Su-chou families, Shen Chou enjoyed two great advantages in his upbringing: the company of many noted scholars, poets and artists among his relatives and their friends, and an abundant education. To these he added talents both scholarly and artistic, along with a passionate desire to read all the books and study all the paintings that were available to him. He learned painting from several teachers, but also by imitating the styles of the artists whom he admired, and he continued throughout his life to do pictures avowedly "in the manner of" various Sung and Yüan masters. He is not, however, a mere eclectic; his are creative reworkings of earlier styles, executed within the limits of his own individual technique and taste.

A comparison of one of his compositions in the manner of Ni Tsan, *Walking With a Staff*, with a landscape by Ni Tsan himself (p. 111) reveals clearly the degree of originality present in one of these "imitations," and is an instructive example of the much-misunderstood Chinese practice of "copying the old masters." Shen Chou preserves the basic Ni Tsan formula: sparse trees growing beside a river, with earthy, lumpy hills beyond. His single addition, an old man walking beneath the trees, is so quiet and

inconspicuous that not even Ni Tsan (who excluded all figures from his landscapes) could have resented the intrusion. Much of the Ni Tsan technique remains also, for example in the characteristic manner of scattering *tien* or dots over the slopes and rocks. For the texture strokes on these slopes, and for contours, Shen Chou replaces Ni Tsan's soft, static application of broad brushstrokes with long, sinuous lines, seemingly lax but charged with a subtle tension; and some of the feeling of repose in the earlier picture is thereby lost. The most meaningful difference, however, is between the two compositions. Out of materials taken over in large part from the Yüan master, Shen Chou has constructed something wholly new, a tightly-knit design on a monumental scale, rendered dynamic by suggestions of instability and surging force in the terrain. The topmost branches of the central, tallest tree are fitted with unnatural neatness into the stream-mouth which evenly divides the rocky shores above; such a nearly axial arrangement, a disturbed symmetry, was unorthodox and even daring for its day. Besides exaggerating for expressive effect two peculiar properties of Ni Tsan's landscape construction, the sharp tilting of the ground plane and the placing of the greatest mass in the upper part of the picture, seemingly without adequate support, Shen Chou introduces another oddity of his own: by avoiding horizontals, even in the shorelines, he gives to the ponderous forms an appearance of threatening to slip sideways.

Shen Chou's was not, however, the tempestuous and passionate spirit of Kuo Hsi and Wang Meng; behind the complexity of design and manipulation of form in this powerful landscape one senses a firmly disciplined intellect, much as one does, for example, in a landscape by Cézanne. The majority of Shen Chou's works are milder and more relaxed than this, and reveal what was the greatest single influence in forming the style of his maturity, the work of Wu Chen. Wu's special blend of naïveté and lyricism, along with his distinctive thick-line drawing, are reflected in the short handscroll titled *Watching the Mid-Autumn Moon*, which Shen Chou painted when he was around sixty years of age. It portrays the painter and three friends gathered to feast and drink wine in a simple shed, which is open on one side to allow them to gaze at the moon. Beyond the sharp-cut river bank, an unbroken expanse of light ink wash stands indiscriminately for water and sky. Light from the full moon, which appears as a pale disc at the far left, mutes the colors of trees and buildings to cool, thin tones. The autumn season, in China as in the West, inspires meditations, usually melancholy ones; Shen Chou's musings on this night, as recorded in the poem he added to the painting, are autumnal in mood:

"When young we heedlessly watch the mid-autumn moon,
Seeing this time as all other time.
With the coming of age respect has grown,
And we do not look lightly
Every time we raise the deep cup to celebrate the feast.
How many mid-autumns can an old man have?
He knows this passing light cannot be held.. "

◄   Shen Chou (1427-1509): Walking with a Staff. Hanging scroll. Ink on paper. (62½×28½")
Palace Museum Collection, Taichung.

Shen Chou (1427-1509): Watching the Mid-Autumn Moon. Handscroll.

The most important among Shen Chou's pupils was Wen Cheng-ming, who was more than forty years his junior. Wen was born and educated in Su-chou, but served for a time at the capital, Peking, as a scholar in the Han-lin Academy, assisting in the compilation of the official history of the Yüan dynasty. He soon abandoned this official career to return to his home in the south, where he devoted the remainder of his long lifetime to literary composition, calligraphy and painting. He became renowned for all three, as well as for the nobility of his character. Like Shen Chou, he studied and imitated the old masters, and worked in various manners. The large picture in the Palace Museum titled *Old Trees by a Cold Waterfall*, painted when he was seventy-nine, represents his finest work in the most dynamic of these manners, one in which Wen the calligrapher strongly impinges upon Wen the painter.

In this display of calligraphic brilliance, delicacy is sacrificed to forcefulness as the brush moves swiftly and fluidly across the surface to build a dense and disordered tangle of pine and cypress trees. Twisting and climbing, they fill most of the tall, narrow frame. Like Wang Meng (p. 114), Wen Cheng-ming drastically limits space in his picture; the trees, constricted in the shallow space before the rock cliff, are all but denied the dimension of depth and flattened into a restless surface pattern. A further extreme from the spacious scenery of Sung painting could hardly be imagined.

We are presented in this picture with something harsh and uningratiating, to which the somber color scheme contributes. It goes beyond the ordinary scholar-painter's

Ink and light colors on paper. (12×53″) Museum of Fine Arts, Boston.

disinclination to please the eye or the facile emotions. Wen Cheng-ming, as revealed in his most characteristic paintings, is a more austere figure than Shen Chou. He was admired for the stern virtues that are symbolized in China by the evergreen trees he portrays here: purity, integrity, unfluctuating devotion to principle. But while a certain affinity exists between such traits in his character and his predilection for pines and cypress, it would be a mistake to suppose that he favored those subjects purely for their symbolic value. The role of symbolism in Chinese painting is often overstressed; the artists were concerned with producing paintings, not symbols to be read intellectually, and with making pictorial and personal statements, not generalized metaphysical or moral ones. A theme was chosen because it was somehow in harmony with the painter's temperament, or with his momentary mood. A Yüan dynasty artist, for example, writes that he always painted bamboo when angry and orchids when happy, and explains that the bristling leaves of the bamboo, sticking outward like spears, allow the expression of anger, while the buoyant and graceful lines of the orchid are suited to feelings of elation. It is expression through form that is involved in this revealing remark, since the bamboo does not ordinarily carry any associations of anger, nor the orchids of happiness. Wen Cheng-ming was partial to winter scenery, both in his own works and in those of earlier artists. He writes in an inscription on a winter landscape of his own: "The lofty scholars and recluses of the past loved to play with the brush, painting landscapes to amuse themselves. Often they did snow scenes; they chose to make use

of that subject in order to embody their feelings of noble loneliness, of freedom from vulgarity." Even when the subject was chosen for its standard connotations, there was still no conflict with the literati painters' ideal of individual expression, since the choice itself reflected the nature and mood of the artist.

With two such creative and prolific artists as Shen Chou and Wen Cheng-ming at its head, the Wu School expanded rapidly, until it included a good many of the leading Su-chou scholars. Among those counted as friends and disciples of Shen and Wen, the best-known are Lu Chih and Ch'en Shun. Both lived unworldly lives, little concerned with practical affairs, absorbed in studies of the Confucian classics; both practiced poetry and calligraphy as well as painting, all on a non-professional status, rounding out the accomplishments considered proper for the ideal scholar-gentleman. Since amateurism in art and such phrases as "play with the brush" carry suggestions of dilettantism for us in the Occident, we may be surprised that so many of these amateurs attained major rank, overshadowing all but a few of the professionals who were their contemporaries. The fact is that their avocations were much more than hobbies or occasional pastimes, and that, in any event, painting as they pursued it required more of poetic sensibility and the connoisseur's familiarity with earlier styles than of the kind of technical skill that comes from laborious practice. Besides, their activities inter-penetrated to a remarkable extent: their training as calligraphers helped to provide them with the mastery of brush technique and sense of design which they needed as painters, and their poetic imagination supplied suitable themes.

The poetic element is especially strong in the work of Lu Chih, for example in his *River Scene in Spring*, a free transposition of the Ni Tsan landscape type into a more lyrical mode. Lu Chih manages to capture the clean, spare quality of Ni Tsan's style even while elaborating the scene with additional hills, trees and buildings, and relieving the ink monochrome with washes of light colors, the combination of pale red-brown and blue-green tones which was favored by adherents of the Wu School. He draws in loose strokes, his brush lightly charged with ink, building his gently swelling forms into slow rhythms. Some contours are traced over with drier, darker ink to give solidity to the structure, but the *tien*, clusters of black dots that are customarily applied as the last stage in the production of a literati school landscape to give a special resonance to the painting surface, are omitted altogether. The season is spring; the river is swollen by melting snows, and the trees put forth sparse new foliage. A man sits immobile at the entrance to his cottage, immersed in the tranquillity of his surroundings. No sound or excitement intrudes upon his contemplation. Lu Chih states in pictorial terms his own ideal, which was shared by many of the traditional poet-scholars: an existence in which one's consciousness becomes like clear water, emotions cleansed, all gross passion refined away, the "dusty world" transcended.

◄   Wen Cheng-ming (1470-1559): Old Trees by a Cold Waterfall. Dated 1549. Hanging scroll.
Ink and colors on silk. (76¼×23¼″) Palace Museum Collection, Taichung.

His *Autumn Colors at Hsün-yang*, a short handscroll illustrating the famous "Lute Song" *(p'i-p'a hsing)* of the T'ang poet Po Chü-i, is in a style more thoroughly Lu Chih's own, although it is not without distant allusions to Ni Tsan and a certain homage to Wen Cheng-ming. In Po Chü-i's narrative poem, composed in 816 when he was serving as a minor official in the south, the poet relates how he was saying farewell to a friend one night in a boat moored at the shore, and heard the sound of a *p'i-p'a*, a kind of lute, being played in a neighboring boat. It proved to be an aging courtesan, once popular in the capital, who was performing the melancholy music. Listening to it, Po Chü-i realized the poignancy of his own long exile from the society of his friends at the capital. Lu Chih aims at approximating the atmosphere of the poem in his painting, rather than at representing its particulars. The red-leafed maple and reeds belong to Po Chü-i's poem, but the narrative details, the boats and figures, are rendered in such miniature scale that they are likely to escape one's notice at first. It is the broad expanse of the river,

Lu Chih (1496-1576): River Scene in Spring. Dated 1535. Section of a handscroll.
Ink and light colors on silk. (H. 14″) Palace Museum Collection, Taichung.

Lu Chih (1496-1576): Autumn Colors at Hsün-yang. Dated 1554. Section of a handscroll.
Ink and light colors on paper. (H. 8¾") Freer Gallery of Art, Washington, D.C.

ruffled with light waves, and the green islets floating upon it, that create an aura of loneliness and nostalgia in harmony with Po Chü-i's theme. The delicacy and refinement of the drawing are hard to match in Ming painting.

Most of the Wu School artists retained in some form the traditional emphasis on linear drawing in their styles, with only occasional essays into those varieties of painting in which line had been all but eliminated. Ch'en Shun was alone in adopting as his speciality the landscape manner of Mi Fu and Mi Yu-jen. His fluency in this manner is brilliantly demonstrated in the handscroll *Mountains in Clouds*, painted, according to his own inscription, in imitation of Mi Yu-jen. By this time, there was nothing startling about the Mi manner in itself; its novelty had worn off long ago, and it had become one of the classical modes. As employed by Ch'en Shun, it takes on a slight air of formalization in spite of its seeming spontaneity. Nothing of the mysterious shapes and modeling of Mi Yu-jen's mountains and mists (p. 92) is to be seen. Ch'en Shun is concerned more with the actual execution of the picture: the wet, impressionistic treatment of the terrain and trees, small idiosyncrasies of brushwork such as the hooked strokes occurring at several places in the clouds, and the rich interplay of color and ink, warm and cool tones mixed with the grey wash.

As a last specimen of Wu School landscape, we offer an enchanting album leaf by Wen Chia, Wen Cheng-ming's son and one of the two most interesting (the other was his nephew Wen Po-jen) of the more than twenty of his descendants who took to painting.

Ch'en Shun (1483-1544): Mountains in Clouds. Dated 1535. Section of a handscroll.
Ink and light colors on paper. (H. 12″) Freer Gallery of Art, Washington, D.C.

It is labeled "In the spirit of verses by Tu Fu," and the verses are written by the artist above his picture: "Blue water flows from afar and falls in a thousand torrents; jade mountains stand in lofty array, cold on their summits." Using this couplet as a point of departure, Wen Chia conjures up a dream vision of strange rain-washed spires and waterfalls streaming down a cliff into a turbulent sea. The flatness of the forms, and the wavering line used for contours, add to the unworldliness of the scene, as do the pale washes of color. The only spots of brighter hues are on the childishly drawn trees. The picture, concealing a high degree of sophistication within an apparent naïveté, fulfills an aesthetic ideal of the Chinese literati painters, who detested ostentatious cleverness and "slickness" above all else. One has only to consider the composition to realize how far removed it is from true simplicity. Like Shen Chou in the landscape reproduced at the beginning of this chapter, Wen Chia avoids the asymmetrical, diagonally arranged design that had long been standard in Chinese painting, and disposes

Wen Chia (1501-1583): Landscape in the Spirit of Verses by Tu Fu. Dated 1576.
Album leaf (upper section, with inscription, not included). Ink and light colors on paper. (w. 14")
Palace Museum Collection, Taichung.

his forms in reference to an imaginary axis bisecting the composition vertically. Precedents for this mode of construction can be found in Northern Sung landscape, for example in the Kuo Hsi picture (p. 36), and in some Yüan compositions, but it was still a departure from the norm. Even more striking is the extreme discrepancy in the angle of view and tilting of the ground plane between the two halves of Wen Chia's picture. The same device, with horizons mismatched at either side of a central mountain mass, was later to be developed by the early Ch'ing master Wang Yüan-ch'i.

Such displays of originality as this were fairly uncommon among the later adherents of the Wu School. Instead, a growing formalization and a gradual loss of creative impetus marked its decline. The dilution of emotional content that may be admired as poetic mildness in works of the masters became unrelieved dullness in those of some lesser followers. Nevertheless, the Wu School in the late Ming period remains a stabilizing force, a strong appeal for rationality, in the face of the rather frantic posturing of the later Che School figures and the violent eccentricities of some of the individualists. If we are tempted to yield to the fashion of dismissing these middle Ming painters as only moderately interesting conservatives and to turn all our attention to the more exciting experiments of later centuries, we might well pause and try to understand why Chinese critics have preferred the disciplined art of Shen Chou, Wen Cheng-ming and their school to the unrestrained styles of such "wild" masters as Hsü Wei, whom we shall encounter in a later chapter. The quiet and subtle taste of the Chinese literati has much to recommend it, if only as a corrective to the sensationalist fondness for the products of neuroticism and aberrations of the artistic temperament, to which the Chinese have occasionally succumbed, although not nearly so regularly as we have in recent times.

Chou Ch'en, T'ang Yin and Ch'iu Ying

13

I

N the early sixteenth century, at a time when the professional and amateur branches of painting were moving in such divergent directions, a trio of highly gifted artists took a position between the two factions and set out to reconcile them. Although the situation was such that they might have seemed foredoomed to failure, they were in fact remarkably successful; two of them are numbered among the half-dozen greatest Ming artists. But theirs were personal triumphs, the flowerings of individual genius; the kinds of painting they practiced demanded a refinement of expression seldom found among the professionals of their age, and a technical equipment equally rare among the amateurs. Therefore, although there were a few lesser artists who are counted as their followers, they can hardly be said to have formed a school. Such terms as "eclectics" and "neo-academics" have been applied to them, but fall short of adequate characterization; nor can they be named for the locality in which they worked, since it was the same Su-chou, or Wu-hsien, that held the Wu School, just then at the height of its prosperity. Nevertheless, these three are best treated together, both because of similarities in their styles and because of their close personal association.

Chou Ch'en, who was probably the oldest of them, is said to have been the teacher of the other two, T'ang Yin and Ch'iu Ying. He was born in Su-chou, learned painting from a master now forgotten, and lived as a professional painter. He received little notice from the critics, who were prejudiced in favor of their own literati class. His connection with T'ang Yin probably brought him into contact with members of the circle of Wen Cheng-ming, to which T'ang Yin had easy access, and a definite "literary" flavor is to be felt in certain of his works. The chief source of his style, however, was the landscape of Li T'ang, who had been strangely neglected since the Sung dynasty. The literati painters professed an admiration for and dependence on the Northern Sung and earlier masters, especially Tung Yüan and Chü-jan; the Che School artists followed the Southern Sung academy, especially the styles of Ma Yüan and Hsia Kuei. It was logical (perhaps too much so to have entered their minds at all) that the painters who attempted to bridge the gulf between these schools should turn to the transitional era of Sung painting, during which the Northern Sung austerity had relaxed but the apogee of the romantic lay yet ahead, the era dominated by Li T'ang.

閒來隱几枕書眠夢入
壺中別有天彷彿若
夷覦面目太墨真訣尋

Probably by Chou Ch'en (fl. c. 1500-1535): Dreaming of Immortality in a Thatched Cottage. Section of a handscroll.

Dreaming of Immortality in a Thatched Cottage, a handscroll in the Freer Gallery of Art, bears an inscription signed "T'ang Yin," but there are sound reasons for doubting the authenticity of this inscription and attributing the painting instead to Chou Ch'en, with several of whose works it agrees closely in style. The affinities with the Li T'ang manner (p. 42) are immediately apparent, in the shapes of rocks and the technique of depicting their surfaces, in the pine trees, in the composition. Other features were probably original with Chou Ch'en, although they appear also in works by T'ang Yin: for example, a fondness for pronounced tonal contrasts, especially on the rocks, where they indicate strong but somewhat arbitrary lights and shadows. The drawing combines a consummate mastery of brush technique with a power of draftsmanship and freedom from mannerism seldom met with in post-Sung painting.

The subject has to do with a poem by Po Chü-i about a man who dreamed he had attained the state of immortality through Taoist practices. The scholar in Chou Ch'en's painting is seen through the open window of his mountaintop cottage, asleep, leaning

Ink and colors on paper. (H. 11⅛") Freer Gallery of Art, Washington, D.C.

on his desk. Then, as the scroll is unrolled further, he appears again in his dream; having sublimated his gross corporeal part, he is floating off to the land of the immortals. We are transported magically from a substantial world, made convincing by the strong modeling of rocks and superb rendering of detail, to a realm of space, an abyss ringed by dim peaks, above which the tiny figure is suspended in midair. Rarely has the handscroll form been so effectively employed.

It may seem odd that the work of a painter of such imagination and ability should have been furnished with false inscriptions and credited to someone else. The reason lies in the far greater popularity of Chou Ch'en's pupil, T'ang Yin. It is even said that T'ang, when the demand for his pictures became greater than he could fulfill, sometimes asked Chou to paint them for him. If true, the story would be another blot on T'ang Yin's already blemished character. His beginnings were brilliant; he took first place twice in provincial examinations, the first time when he was only fifteen years old. Su-chou scholarly society befriended and supported him, and at the age of twenty-eight he set off for the capital with high hopes, to take the state examination that was the entrance to a career as government official. Again he passed in first place; but it was later disclosed that a playboy friend had bribed the servant of the examiner to get advance information of the essay subjects; T'ang Yin was involved in the ensuing scandal, and degraded. Finding himself thus barred from the standard vocation of the literatus, and, unlike Wen Cheng-ming and others, too poor to live in elegant retirement on private means, he settled into an in-between existence, selling paintings when he needed money, forgetting the bitterness of his disgrace in the taverns and pleasure quarters of Su-chou one day, transcending it through Ch'an Buddhist meditation the next. Throughout all this he kept the friendship of that paragon of virtue Wen Cheng-ming, who admonished him in vain for his profligacy.

Artistically, too, he stands between; some of his works are in a thoroughly scholarly style and taste, others follow the more professional Li T'ang-derived manner of Chou Ch'en. One of the finest of the latter kind is a handscroll in the Palace Museum, *Secluded Fishermen on an Autumn River*. In a poetic passage toward the center of the composition, two scholar-fishermen relax in their boats, one trailing his foot in the water and playing a flute, the other keeping time by clapping. Fallen red leaves drift on the waves and lie scattered on the rocks. The autumnal mood of the scene is set by imagined sound, the melancholy notes of the flute blending with the soft plash of the waterfall behind. The harmony of colors is exceptionally lovely, and reveals a different attitude toward color from that current among the literati artists, who generally use it only decoratively, in standardized schemes, and often as an unessential embellishment to ink monochrome painting. Washes of blue-green and red-brown tones help to give substance to the rocks, especially to the large boulder at the left; its texture is conveyed by short strokes in ink, derived from Li T'ang's "axe-cut *ts'un*" and applied, like Li's, with a partially dry "squeezed brush" *(ts'a-pi)*. The result is a more convincing rendition of mass and solidity than is common in Ming dynasty painting, which ordinarily pays little attention either to natural textures or to the plastic properties of the surfaces they cover. The elaborate, often restless modeling of surfaces was a special preoccupation of T'ang Yin; it turns to a mannerism in the works of his imitators and, to a lesser degree, in T'ang's own paintings: the rocky cliff to the right of the waterfall, for example, is covered with pale strokes that hardly function as modeling at all, but merely repeat, in their angularity and the rhythm of their spacing, the pattern of waves on the river below. The drawing is fluid and elegant; a Ming critic speaks of T'ang Yin's brushwork as "more refined" than that of Li T'ang, but this statement may be regarded as a reflection of the prejudice of a period when brushwork was more esteemed for its own sake, and a recognition of T'ang's brushline as more suave, and more conspicuous, than that of the Sung master.

T'ang Yin's small picture titled *Clearing after Snow in a Mountain Pass* is patterned upon another Li T'ang painting type, the monumental landscape. The season is early winter, probably just after the first snowfall, since leaves are still on the trees; the time early evening, as heavily laden oxcarts approach the end of their day's journey, a village

Ch'iu Ying (c. 1510-1551): Passing a Summer Day beneath Banana Palms. Section of a hanging scroll (cropped at top and bottom). Ink and colors on paper. (w. 39″) Palace Museum Collection, Taichung.

T'ang Yin (1470-1523): Secluded Fishermen on an Autumn River. Inscription by a friend, dated 1523. Section of a handscroll. Ink and colors on silk. (H. 11½") Palace Museum Collection, Taichung.

in the pass. Like Kuo Hsi in his *Early Spring*, T'ang Yin uses delicate gradations of ink tone to suggest a few local areas of haze filling pockets in the terrain, but otherwise presents his scene with the utmost sharpness, as viewed through the clear, cold wintry air. In place of atmospheric perspective, a system of piled diagonals establishes the desired depth, and the painting seems unusually spacious for a Ming work. T'ang Yin attempts, with considerable success, to recover the firm structure and solidity of form found in Northern Sung landscape, perhaps in deliberate opposition to the flatter, less substantial constructions of the Wu School literati.

Such paintings as these, along with others in his "literary" manner, were no doubt admired and purchased by discerning men of Su-chou, and prized by later connoisseurs. The pictures which brought him his greatest popular success, however, were colorful figure studies, especially of beautiful women. They seem to us rather vapid today, but are much praised by Chinese writers, who remark slyly that his intimate acquaintance with the courtesans of Su-chou must have given him a special competence in the portrayal

画阁雪霁推入稠　轻载驢騾
重载牛斜斗店前山積鐡皶
墓後不酒徑油晋昌唐寅作

T'ang Yin (1470-1523): Clearing after Snow in a Mountain Pass. Hanging scroll.
Ink and light colors on silk. (27½×14¾″) Palace Museum Collection, Taichung.

of feminine beauty. Ch'iu Ying, the other student of Chou Ch'en, was equally popular for pictures of this kind, and the two younger men founded together (probably without intending to do so) what is perhaps better regarded as an industry than as a school, made up of hosts of hack artists who labored at decorative paintings, book illustrations, erotic works and the like, all ostensibly in the manners of T'ang and Ch'iu. A good proportion of the imitations were furnished with "signatures" of the masters, and they still abound. Ch'iu Ying has suffered especially from being burdened with spurious pictures; the first task of anyone seeking to understand and appraise him, in fact, is to clear away an accretion of innumerable forgeries, works of minor followers, dull and academic productions misattributed to him. This mass of mediocrities has until fairly recently clouded his reputation, giving the false impression that he was an industrious but hardly imaginative artist. He was much more than that; seeing his genuine works, many of which are not yet widely known, we can credit him with sensitivity as well as skill, and with a considerable power of invention as well, although this last was not his forte.

Most of the styles in which Ch'iu Ying worked are based in some way on T'ang and Sung painting. His scenes of women's quarters in the palace, for example, are in the long tradition extending back by way of Ch'ien Hsüan and Chou Wen-chü to the T'ang masters Chang Hsüan and Chou Fang. Perhaps the finest of his few surviving works in this genre is the long handscroll *Spring Morning in the Han Palace*. A court painter is engaged in portraying an empress or imperial concubine, in the portion reproduced here, while her maids cluster around them like brightly colored birds, and two palace eunuchs stand guard outside. This is just the kind of painting for which Ch'iu was best known; in the standard biographical sketch of him, for example, we read: "Ch'iu's paintings were beautiful and elegant, full of delicate and graceful detail. The brushwork was so refined that the pictures looked as though they had been carved in jade... He was particularly skilled in painting gentlemen and ladies; they were all brilliantly colored and looked alive. If Chou Fang came back, he could not surpass Ch'iu Ying." Our admiration may stop short of agreement with this final remark; Ch'iu's figures lack the naturalness of posture, and his faces the character, of Chou Fang's. But delicate, graceful and jadelike they surely are, and the reasons for their popularity are easily apparent. Transmitted by imitations in woodblock prints of the late Ming period, they influenced profoundly the Ukiyo-e school, the popular art of the Edo period in Japan.

Also in an archaistic mode, Ch'iu Ying painted blue-and-green landscapes, ostensibly based on the T'ang masters but actually more dependent on Ch'ien Hsüan's transformations of this manner. Excellent examples are to be seen in both the Museum of Fine Arts, Boston and the Nelson Gallery, Kansas City. His preoccupation with the past, and the classicistic spirit of much of his work, was no doubt the fruit of his close association with the literati, especially with the circle of Wen Cheng-ming. It was through them, and through such local collectors as the famous Hsiang Yüan-pien, that he was able to see the old paintings which were the models for his archaistic works; such paintings were all kept in private collections, public museums being unheard of in pre-modern China. The literati painters praised his pictures, often adding laudatory inscriptions to

Ch'iu Ying (c. 1510-1551): Spring Morning in the Han Palace. Section of a handscroll.
Ink and colors on silk. (H. 12″) Palace Museum Collection, Taichung.

them. The allusions to old styles in their own works were more distant, partly because
they lacked the technique to reproduce them as accurately as Ch'iu could, but also
because of their more individualistic aims; nevertheless, they recognized a similarity
of approach. Thus, although Ch'iu's whole genius was directed toward painting— he was
not, that is, a scholar, poet or calligrapher—he moved among the literati, and evidently
tried to conform to their aesthetic standards in some of his work, as did Chou Ch'en and
T'ang Yin. One might say, were it not too neat and narrow an explanation, that the
stylistic variety within the paintings of these three men mirrors the whole multi-layered
society of Su-chou.

Close to the "literary" pole within Ch'iu Ying's *œuvre* are three huge figures-in-landscape compositions which survive from a set of four, corresponding to the four seasons. The summer scene, *Passing a Summer Day beneath Banana Palms*, is preserved in the Palace Museum collection, along with one other from the set. It portrays two scholars sitting on the ground, in the shade of banana palms and tall rocks, escaping

Ch'iu Ying (c. 1510-1551): Landscape in the Manner of Li T'ang. Section of a handscroll. Ink and colors on paper. (H. 10″) Freer Gallery of Art, Washington, D.C.

the heat. One plucks a kind of banjo, the other listens; a servant boy prepares flowers in a bronze vase nearby. Those qualities which bear most upon the narrative import of the scene are emphasized: the coolness of the shady retreat by a predominance of blue and green tones, its isolation by the foreground boulders, which are felt as a block by the spectator. The painter has carried his scholarly pose to the point of signing "Playfully drawn by Ch'iu Ying," a disclaimer of serious intent that was common among the amateurs, who typically asserted a free-and-easy aesthetic attitude, but seems odd in a professional. Despite his simulation of a relaxed manner (note the scribbly texturing of the rocks), Ch'iu Ying never lapses from his customary elegance of form and excellence of drawing; nor is the line, however swift and fluid, anywhere allowed to become as rough or imprecise as it does in Che School works. A composition on this scale, executed throughout with such absolute assurance, is the performance of a great painter, which Ch'iu Ying surely was.

He was so obviously a great painter, in fact, as to pose a dilemma for literati critics after his time. T'ang Yin was no problem; however wayward, he was still a scholar and a gentleman of a sort. But how could they, consistent with their principles ("the quality of the painting reflects the quality of the man"), give full approval to an "artisan-painter," as the professionals were condescendingly called, of no special eminence otherwise, who was besides given to immodest displays of technical proficiency? On the other hand, it was difficult to find a basis on which to disparage Ch'iu's pictures. One charge made against him is over-elaboration—a contemporary critic remarks that he "could not refrain from adding feet when painting a snake." Such a charge might be brought against one of Ch'iu's masterpieces, the long handscroll in the Freer Gallery of Art painted in the Li T'ang manner. The profusion of anecdotal detail, the careful application of spots of bright color, the precision of the drawing, bring it perilously near to fussiness; few post-Sung artists could have handled such a composition without falling into academicism. But under the enlivening brush of Ch'iu Ying it sustains a high pitch of interest, even excitement, from beginning to end, and individual passages, such as the cliff-enclosed ravine in our detail, have a fairyland quality of ideal beauty.

To infuse new life into the old, conservative styles and techniques was not, at this late date, an easy task. Chou Ch'en, T'ang Yin and Ch'iu Ying were perhaps the last artists to accomplish it with complete success. For a few decades, these three restored to professional painting some qualities it had lacked since the Sung dynasty, notably the kind of discipline in both technique and taste that prevented such vices as showy brushwork and meretricious appeal, and a revived respect for that accuracy and clarity of presentation that had been the ideal of the Sung academy. But these reforms were short-lived, scarcely surviving the reformers. Even so, their influence in other directions was far-reaching and salutary; the indebtedness of Ch'en Hung-shou (p. 152) to Ch'iu Ying, or Tao-chi (p. 181) to T'ang Yin, is no less real for not having been acknowledged. All three may be credited, also, with stimulating a new interest in pictorial content, narrative and descriptive, and thus helping to counteract the severe limitation of themes which threatened to impoverish the literati school; for, while concentration on a narrow range of motifs may be allowable and even necessary in the truly creative masters, leaving them more free to pursue their individual formal concerns, it can make the works of their unimaginative followers seem even more drearily repetitive than they otherwise would. Most important of all, these brilliant artists demonstrated once more a truth that was constantly being doubted and denied in the later centuries in China: that technical skill is in no way incompatible with genius, nor is dullness the inevitable outcome of careful craftsmanship.

14

THE proliferation of separate stylistic currents or schools of painting in the late Ming dynasty is one of the many astonishing features of that fascinating period. It resembles the modern Western situation in this way, and also in being an age of endless discussion of principles, of the formulation of theories and their application to painting of the past, in an attempt to categorize and evaluate all that had gone before. The painters themselves, affected by this intellectual activity and as often as not participating in it, adhered to one or another faction according to their beliefs and preferences, or, to some degree, according to the locality in which they worked. At the same time, some of the most interesting figures of this period remained relatively isolated, more so than painters had tended to be since the Yüan dynasty, and are properly to be classified as individualists.

Dominating the age stands the imposing figure of Tung Ch'i-ch'ang. As a high official, one of the leading scholars and calligraphers of his day, and by far the most eminent authority on painting, he was a man of enormous self-confidence, not to say self-esteem. In addition to his voluminous published writings on painting, in which he restates and elaborates the tenets of literati painting theory, he composed hundreds of colophons for particular pictures, delivering dogmatic judgements and making attributions that, for better or worse, carry considerable weight even today. Many of them still seem very perceptive; others may strike us as arbitrary—it was Tung, to take an example, who decided that the fan-shaped picture reproduced on p. 81 is a work of Chao Po-chü, although there is no stylistic or other evidence that it has anything at all to do with Chao, and some to the contrary. Tung Ch'i-ch'ang undertook also to codify painting styles, and classified the old masters according to his famous system of the "Northern and Southern Schools," a system too complex and controversial to be treated here; we can only remark that, although not explicitly designed to do so, it glorified the literati painting tradition and belittled the academicians and professionals, especially the Che School painters. In short, he attempted to bring the whole history and art of painting into a state of order satisfactory to himself and convincing to his contemporaries. He succeeded so well that most books about painting written in China after his time are strongly under his influence.

In his own painting, he submits nature to the same kind of systematization; he observes, analyzes, compares it with the visions of earlier artists, borrows what he pleases from them, but in the end reorganizes the visual material according to personal principles. Although his attitude was intellectual, it would be a mistake to regard his pictures purely as objectifications of his theories. Forms, not concepts, occupied Tung Ch'i-ch'ang the painter. One may find his works uncomfortable, with their deliberate dissonances, but one cannot deny their power, or continue to assume (as many Western scholars once did) that the oddness of his style is the product of incompetence.

◄   Tung Ch'i-ch'ang (1555-1636): Autumn Landscape. Hanging scroll. Ink and light colors on silk. (56×23½″)
Nü Wa Chai Collection.

Sun K'o-hung (1532-1610): The Moon Rises, from Elegant Diversions for Leisure Hours. Section of a handscroll. Ink and light colors on paper. (H. 11″) Palace Museum Collection, Taichung.

Ch'en Hung-shou (1599-1652): Boating on the Lake. Album leaf. Ink and colors on paper. (13⅛×10¾″)
J. P. Dubosc Collection, Lugano.

The autumn landscape in the Nü Wa Chai collection, one of his finest paintings, uses the standard Ni Tsan compositional formula (cf. p. 111). Unlike Shen Chou (p. 126), who preserves much of the Ni Tsan technique but uses it to construct a landscape on a very different pattern, Tung retains the basic design but renders it in a technique totally unlike Ni Tsan's. If we search for sources of the style, it must be in such pictures as the *Green Hills and White Clouds* of Kao K'o-kung (p. 104), in which some precedent for the strangely sleek forms, the repetition of mound shapes and bulging, round-topped cones, may be seen. Tung's composition is at once more monumental and less stable, with its leaning masses in a state of uncertain equilibrium. Neither the somber coloring nor the drawing of the trees, themselves devoid of charm, helps to relieve the starkness of the scene. Tung Ch'i-ch'ang avoids anecdotal content as scrupulously as Ni Tsan, and the exclusion of figures from his landscapes is nearly as rigorous. If we believe with the literati theorists that the painting reflects the man, we receive an impression of Tung as a high-principled and austere personality.

Some painters, in the same period, continued to work in the milder and more lyrical mode of Shen Chou and the Wu School. Among these was Sun K'o-hung, an older contemporary and friend of Tung Ch'i-ch'ang, who is classed with Tung in the Hua-t'ing School, named after the town near Su-chou where they both lived. He was a scholar, collector and antiquarian, in whose life painting played a smaller part than it did in Tung Ch'i-ch'ang's. His handscroll made up of twenty scenes representing *Elegant Diversions for Leisure Hours* illustrates once more how far a poetic sensibility can compensate for the lack of any great technical proficiency. Sun K'o-hung, without the temperament to undertake the grand explorations of the major individualist masters, nevertheless joins in the experimental spirit of the age to develop a personal manner reminiscent of the color woodcut, combining heavy line with pale, flat washes of color. In the section titled *The Moon Rises*, the cool tones of early evening moonlight on the trunks of the *wu-t'ung* trees and on the rocks are admirably suggested, although not by any means accurately reproduced. The composition is unhackneyed, and drawn with an artless air—the fact that the scholar gazes from his open window in a direction quite away from the moon he is supposedly observing does not disturb the artist at all. Despite some obvious influence of Shen Chou in style and theme, the picture as a whole seems strikingly fresh and original.

Some of the late Ming painters were involved, to greater or lesser degrees, in the political feuds that weakened the central administration in the late sixteenth and early seventeenth centuries, and many more were affected by the rebellions of the last years of the dynasty, and by its final collapse before the invading Manchus. It may be that a certain inwardness of feeling in painting of this age, and the fond reversions to an idealized antiquity to be felt in some of its styles, express, like the same features in Yüan painting, a desire for escape that could not be adequately realized in actuality. The works of Ch'en Hung-shou, for example, would never lead one to suppose that he was a man susceptible of involvement in the fortunes of governments, but he was in fact involved, although perhaps against his will. Born in Chekiang Province, he painted from

枝枝葉葉自成排嫩嫩粘粘
向上裁信手拂來東非
著意些睛是雨憶人猜

Hsü Wei (1521-1593): Bamboo. Section of a handscroll. Ink on paper. (H. 12¹³/₁₆")
Freer Gallery of Art, Washington, D.C.

Chang Feng (fl. c. 1645-1673): Gazing at a Red-leafed Maple across a Ravine. Dated 1660. ▶
Hanging scroll (cropped at top). Ink and light colors on paper. (W. 17¾") Yamato Bunka-kan, Osaka.

boyhood, developing an accomplished technique and a very individual manner based
in a curious way on antique styles. When his fame reached the Ming emperor, he was
invited to the Peking court, where he served a short term around the year 1640 in an
official position, although not as a court painter proper. In 1642, he was nominated
to the Academy of Learning and accepted, but declined the rank of "painter-in-atten-
dance" that was also offered him. Perhaps the general castigation of "academy painters"

by such contemporary scholars as Tung Ch'i-ch'ang affected his decision to refuse. The reports on his movements during the confused period of the Manchu conquest are vague and somewhat contradictory; one story has it that he was imprisoned upon the fall of Nanking in 1645, but released because of his artistic eminence by the Manchus, who were on the whole reasonable and lenient as conquerors. He entered the Buddhist priesthood for a time, then returned to his home, where he died in 1652.

Most of the archaistically-inclined painters of his time talked grandly of T'ang and pre-T'ang styles, but what we find in their works are only fairly standardized references to the manners of certain canonical Sung and Yüan masters. Ch'en Hung-shou, almost alone among painters of his time, made a genuine study of pre-Sung painting, and the results of it are to be seen in his own works. In the landscape album leaf we reproduce, the simply-drawn hills seen across the water are quoted from T'ang landscape, as are the composition and the sharp-cut, blue-and-green rocks. Such allusions to antiquity do not, however, account for the special quality of Ch'en Hung-shou's work, which is not at all derivative in the ordinary sense of the word. Through playful distortions of form and space, quirks of drawing, linear eccentricities, he creates something thoroughly original and personal. The emotional content of his pictures is as complex as their styles, and as far removed from the straightforward statements of early painting. The melancholy lady gazing from an upstairs window recalls the themes of many poignant T'ang poems, but this motif functions here as a once-removed reference to feeling, rather than as a direct expression of feeling. It does not, and is not intended to, ring entirely true. Such an oblique mode of expression is familiar to us in the modern Occident, for example in the subtle, semi-facetious plays on romantic style in the music of certain modern French composers, which is somehow akin, in its bitter-sweet flavor, to such paintings as this.

Ch'en Hung-shou was best known for his figure paintings, most of them imaginary portraits and representations of historical or Buddhist subjects. Outstanding among these is a handscroll illustrating the long poem titled "Homecoming" by T'ao Yüan-ming, the same fourth century poet who is probably portrayed in the anonymous Sung picture on p. 63. T'ao was fond of wine, music and chrysanthemums, and he is shown enjoying all three in the first section of Ch'en's scroll: seated on a rock, he inhales the fragrance of a bunch of his favorite flowers, his lute beside him, a bowl of wine on a flat stone in front. For the costume of the figure, Ch'en has returned to the stylistic stage of the Ku K'ai-chih painting (p. 14), when drapery was drawn with continuous lineament in long curves, and revealed little about the body beneath. The drawing of the rock is based closely on the T'ang manner which may be seen in the *Emperor Ming-huang's Journey to Shu* (pp. 28 and 57), so closely—even to the particular movement of line and the "nail-head" endings—as to indicate that that picture, or a very similar one, must have been known to Ch'en Hung-shou. The addition of light shading to the fine, even lineament and thin color wash also agrees with early styles. But again, the whole effect of the picture is personal and novel; the insistent rhythms of repeated line are Ch'en's own, and there are hints of the distortion that makes others of his figure paintings distinctly grotesque.

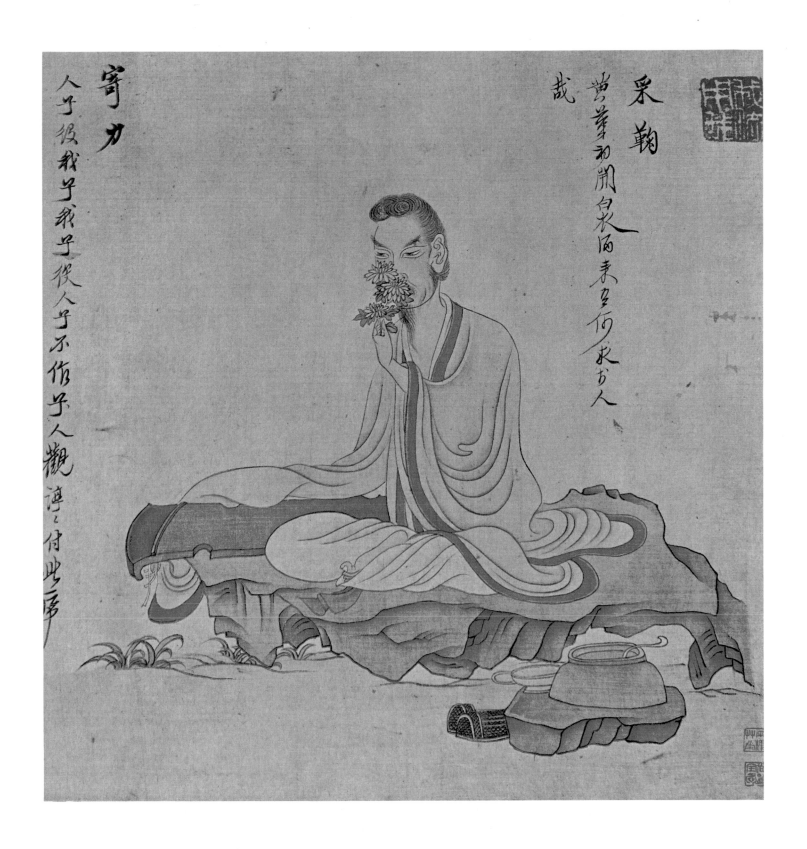

Ch'en Hung-shou (1599-1652): Illustrations to the "Homecoming" Ode of T'ao Yüan-ming. Section of a handscroll.
Ink and light color on silk. (H. 11¾") Honolulu Academy of Arts.

157

Pretending to aim at recapturing the ingenuous air of painting that seemed to his age primitive and unspoiled, he deliberately overdoes the element of awkwardness, revealing thereby, paradoxically perhaps, an extreme point of sophistication.

As final specimens of late Ming painting, we have juxtaposed two works separated by seven or eight decades in time; the Chang Feng picture, in fact, was painted in the early part of the following dynasty, the Ch'ing. Both are executed in a bold and free brushwork, which goes back ultimately to the rough brush techniques of the *i-p'in* or "untrammeled" manner of the T'ang and Sung painters; in both, the movements of the brush seem sometimes to have been dictated more by expressionist than by representational motives, and certain strokes have no descriptive function at all. But these common features, significant as they are, clearly have not decided the expressive character of the two pictures, which employ the same calligraphic looseness of brushwork for very different purposes. The Hsü Wei bamboo appears to be the product of a furious attack of brush on paper, a swiftness not entirely under control, as if the excited artist had been impatient to exteriorize some force pressing upon his mind and could not take time for thought. The Chang Feng picture, although there is as much arbitrariness in the drawing, conveys a gentler and poetic mood. The line is relaxed where Hsü Wei's is tense, slow-moving where Hsü's is impetuous. We may account for these differences as we please, or deny any need to account for them at all. For the Chinese critics, however, they are to be explained in only one way: by reference to the individual temperaments of the painters themselves.

Hsü Wei was, like T'ang Yin, a child prodigy, showing outstanding literary ability by the time he was ten. Attaching himself as secretary to an ambitious governor, he rose rapidly to prominence, but fell even more rapidly when the governor was imprisoned for political intrigue. Hsü feared for his own life, and pretended madness. His behavior had always been extremely odd, so his performance was no doubt convincing. He escaped prison on that occasion, but not on the next, when he was convicted of murder, having beaten his second wife to death. He attempted suicide while in prison, but was unsuccessful, and a friend finally secured his release. After a stay in the capital, he returned to his home in Chekiang, poor, ill, and embittered. He drank to excess, managed a precarious living by selling his paintings and calligraphy, and treated most of his fellow townspeople with rudeness and contempt. "People thought he was too strange," we read in his biography, "and nobody liked him." He died penniless at the age of seventy-three.

Much less is known about the life of Chang Feng, partly because he was never so famous as Hsü Wei, but also because his was a less colorful and eventful life, and so less rewarding for the chronicler. He was a minor official until the fall of the Ming, but then, like so many late Ming intellectuals, retired into semi-poverty to avoid serving the Manchus. Noblemen and high dignitaries entertained him in the hope of being presented with one of his landscapes or figure pictures. "He lived in peace with everybody, never showing bad temper, because he was by nature very retiring..." says one writer. "He found satisfaction within himself."

With these facts and opinions about the painters in our minds, and the pictures before us, we may return to the question of what relationship, if any, there is between them. To what extent does the vehemence of expression in the bamboo picture, that is, derive from the tormented and neurotic person of Hsü Wei, or the relaxed charm of the composition titled *Gazing at a Red-leafed Maple across a Ravine* from the amiable Chang Feng? To no extent at all, reply adherents of some current Western aesthetic theories, which hold that the feeling embodied in a work of art need never have been experienced by the artist himself, and that the artist is in fact more or less irrelevant to his work. The contention of the Chinese critics was exactly the opposite. A man cannot apply brush to paper, they believed, without revealing something of his innermost self. Given the facts and the paintings, they would not have hesitated long before deciding which could have been done by a man who had murdered his wife, and which by one well adjusted and well liked.

15

WITH the end of the Ming and beginning of the Ch'ing dynasty, Chinese painting entered a third phase. During the first, which had lasted until the eleventh century, it had been predominantly a professional tradition, made up of various schools but preserving a certain uniformity of style and attitude, from which individual deviations were relatively minor. The foundation of the literati branch of painting by Su Tung-p'o and his circle in the late Northern Sung period began the second, a long period of schism between two great movements, marked by the steady rise of one of them, that of the scholar-amateurs, and the decline of the other, that of the professional artists. By the seventeenth century the contest was ended; the professional schools of painting were quite stagnant, devoid of imagination and impetus, and merit no more serious attention now than they received from their contemporary critics, which was virtually none at all. The literati tradition, meanwhile, had split into divergent currents, and from this time onward the polarities of orthodoxy v. individualism, imitation v. innovation, were to be found within this literati tradition itself. The rich diversity of Chinese painting was sustained.

There appears to be a correlation, of the most general kind, between the artistic inclinations of early Ch'ing painters and their modes of response to the Manchu conquest: many of those termed "individualists," as we shall see in the next chapter, retired into Buddhist or Taoist temples and became monks, while the "orthodox" artists typically felt less urge toward withdrawal, and either went into dignified seclusion in their homes, or, ih many cases, accepted positions in the new administration after a few decades had passed. As painters, they were mostly followers of Tung Ch'i-ch'ang, who, although not by any means a conservative in his own paintings, had been so authoritative in his choice of styles, so dogmatic in his opinions and uncompromising in his judgements, as to found a new orthodoxy, which allowed certain kinds of brushwork, certain compositions, certain attitudes, and strictly forbade others. The output of Tung's following in the generation after him may seem to Occidental eyes tamely homogeneous. Chinese connoisseurs, more sensitive to stylistic subtleties within their own tradition, could recognize and admire (to take a not untypical case) a landscape by Wang Shih-min following Tung Ch'i-ch'ang in imitating Wang Meng's interpretation of the Tung Yüan manner.

Wang Shih-min (1592-1680): Landscape in the Manner of Chao Meng-fu. Dated 1670. Album leaf.
Ink and colors on paper. (10⅝×14⅝″) C. C. Wang Collection, New York.

The leaders of the orthodox school in this generation were the two older of the so-called Four Wangs, Wang Shih-min and Wang Chien. Wang Shih-min came from a prominent family of scholars, and studied painting under Tung Ch'i-ch'ang while still young. He held an official position in the Ming government, but retired and lived quietly after the fall of the dynasty, writing and painting, entertaining artists and scholars, teaching pupils. He bought or borrowed pictures by his favorite artists whenever he could, in order to study and copy them and so enrich his own stock of techniques and motives. He followed Tung Ch'i-ch'ang in esteeming above all the Yüan masters, especially Huang Kung-wang, whose method of building the picture slowly, stroke on stroke and wash on wash, as well as his choice of plain, unexciting subjects, had a

Wu Li (1632-1718): Boating on the River below a Buddhist Temple. Album leaf.
Ink and light colors on paper. (15⅝×10½″) Palace Museum Collection, Taichung.

profound appeal to the quiet taste of the Ch'ing orthodox painters. The salient qualities of Wang Shih-min's style, and that of many of his associates and followers, derive more from Huang than from any other early painter: a denseness of surface, achieved through close interweaving of brushstrokes; blends of wet and dry in the application of ink; a technical consistency that was always in danger of falling into monotony when production outran inspiration. Characteristic of this school is the avoidance of firm, continuous line and simple surfaces; linear contours are constantly disrupted with heavy applications of *tien*, small strokes of varying shape, and surfaces are roughened with uneven washes and texture strokes.

Wang Shih-min's landscape after Chao Meng-fu is from an album of pictures done "in imitation of" various masters. The making of such albums, as demonstrations of the painter's repertory, had been popular among the literati artists since the time of Shen Chou. The "Chao Meng-fu" elements are not easily detectable; the archaistic clouds, heavy green color and cramped, tortuous composition evidently refer to Chao's reworking of a T'ang or Five Dynasties landscape type. There is no sense of space or atmosphere, no real body to the forms, no feeling of grandeur in nature, nothing that can be called skillful drawing. The fact that one finds it easiest to characterize painting of this kind in such negative statements is itself significant, since much of the style is in fact the end product of a long process of stripping away, in which all that the artists disapproved or found uncongenial—all obvious blandishments, easy effects and recognizable technical tricks, all elements designed to charm, to appeal, to impress, to make the picture immediately admirable or likeable—had been ruthlessly eliminated. This is not to argue that all the flatness and awkward touches in the painting are intentional. But the question of how far such an amateur as Wang Shih-min could have moved in the direction of illusionistic rendering of three-dimensional space and form, or of more representational drawing, had he wished to do so, is not only unanswerable but really irrelevant as well, since his paintings were clearly executed with other aims than these in mind. Their positive virtues are not so easily isolated and described as their negative qualities; words of praise for their richness of texture, or (to fall back on Chinese criteria) harmony and resonance of surface, will be all but meaningless to anyone who does not admire them to begin with. It is unlikely that painting of this school will ever be popular outside China. Even the Japanese, for all their concern with Chinese painting, have never quite seen the point of it, and it lacks the simplicity and boldness of design, the candid air and expressive transparence, which make some exotic arts attractive to us today, and which we sometimes mistake for marks of artistic excellence.

The works of Wang Shih-min's contemporary Wang Chien are often so similar to his own that it requires a sharp eye to distinguish them. More individual manners appear in the following generation, in the two younger of the Four Wangs, Wang Hui and Wang Yüan-ch'i, and in two other artists, Wu Li and Yün Shou-p'ing, who are commonly grouped with the Wangs as the Six Great Orthodox Masters of the Early Ch'ing. Wang Hui, the best known of them, was enormously prolific without being outstandingly inventive. He began as a highly gifted eclectic, passed through a relatively fertile middle period, and ended by turning out a profusion of paintings in a monotonous manner, without, it would appear, expending much thought or feeling on more than a few of them. His work thus ranges from very good at best to dreary at worst. The less abundant output of Wu Li, while it also varies in quality, sustains on the whole a higher level of interest. The two men were almost exactly the same age, and both studied under Wang Shih-min.

The life of Wu Li has held a special attraction for Occidental scholars, because he was converted to Christianity at the age of fifty, entering the Jesuit order. Chinese records state that he visited Western countries, but the fact is that he never traveled further than the southern coastal island of Macao, on which there was a Portuguese colony. There he received religious instruction for a number of years. Upon his return to the mainland, he was sent as a missionary to Shanghai and Chia-ting. He continued to paint after his return, but only occasionally, his main energies being devoted to his duties as a Catholic father. This reduction of output was probably the only effect that his adoption of the Christian faith had on his painting; no trace of western influence appears in it.

Like all the other orthodox masters of his time, he worked often "in old styles." The manner most original to Wu Li himself is that represented in our plate, a leaf from one of his albums ostensibly done in homage to Sung and Yüan masters. It is a dry and intellectual kind of painting, which, in the Chinese phrase, "used ink as sparingly as if it were gold." Certain forms in it are the artist's personal property: peaks and ridges twist in distinctive ways, and the large masses are made up of smaller, bulging shapes, often oddly pointed at the top or side, which are thus made to thrust in particular opposed directions and so to give tension to the whole body. Some precedent for this mode of construction can be found in the works of Tung Ch'i-ch'ang. The insistent repetition of rows of *tien* along the contours of rocks and the edges of tree trunks, giving a furry texture to these bodies, is a feature derived from Wang Shih-min and shared with Wang Hui, who carried it to a point of excess. Here, it does not detract from the crispness of the composition.

The youngest of the group, and perhaps the most original of them all, was Wang Shih-min's grandson Wang Yüan-ch'i. He studied painting under his grandfather, and became a high official, placed in charge of the imperial collection of painting and calligraphy by the K'ang-hsi Emperor (reigned 1662-1722). Although never a court painter in the true sense—he held a much higher administrative rank—he dominated the court academy during the latter decades of his life. Wang Yüan-ch'i perpetuated what had been one of the main strengths of the literati tradition: the capacity for using old forms and techniques in fresh ways, taking advantage of the discoveries of predecessors and the evolution of centuries, but utilizing them for personal statements. This variety of traditionalism, which seems peculiarly Confucian in intent, might be likened to a conservative poet's or prose writer's employment of the rich language of literary English, with its established imagery and formal devices, for his own expressive needs and new

Wang Yüan-ch'i (1642-1715): River Landscape, in the Manner of Ni Tsan. Dated 1704. Hanging scroll.
Ink and light colors on paper. (37½×19⅞″) J. P. Dubosc Collection, Lugano.

content. The basic material of Wang Yüan-ch'i's pictures is orthodox: the dry, dragged brushline over light, wet underdrawing, the gradual building of form by accumulation of strokes, limited areas of wash tying it all together. His coloring, although sometimes put to unusually effective use in defining forms, remains within the confines of the orthodox literati school, combining pale blue-green and red-brown tones with the ink in subtle harmonies. His compositions, however, make his classification as "orthodox" quite meaningless, since they are among the most imaginative and daring in all of Chinese painting.

In one of his two inscriptions on the landscape in the Ni Tsan manner reproduced here, he writes that he painted it after his memory of a picture by his grandfather Wang Shih-min, which had been done in imitation of Tung Ch'i-ch'ang. And behind all this, of course, was Ni Tsan, the ultimate source—ultimate, that is, until we go further and trace the sources of Ni Tsan's style. That a painting burdened with so many layers of stylistic allusion can have room left for originality may seem unlikely, but it is in fact highly original. Wang Yüan-ch'i's large masses, like those of Tung Ch'i-ch'ang and Wu Li, are constituted of smaller bodies, but without the same sense of cohesion. The central mesa appears fragmented into a pile of lumpy boulders, heaped against the flat-topped, columnar core. More bizarre motives include the leaning rock near the shore and the absurdly low pavilion. Wang Yüan-ch'i's paramount concern, however, apart from the ever-major one of brushwork, was for the formal construction of the picture —the organization of dense or empty areas, balance or unbalance of masses, repetition of lines and shapes. Like Shen Chou in his *Walking with a Staff* (p. 126), he takes the Ni Tsan composition as a starting point and plays upon it with complex deviations and distortions, including some inherent in his model—the irregularly tilted ground plane, the ponderous mass at the top "supported" by curving trees—but also some of his own, such as the intricate off-symmetrical arrangement, and the fantastically mismatched horizons at the two sides of the picture.

Jean Pierre Dubosc, who was one of the first Occidental scholars to arrive at a real understanding of the very specialized values of this school of painting, has likened Wang Yüan-ch'i to Cézanne, and the comparison is both stimulating and valid. Like Cézanne, Wang protested always that his art was founded in nature, and recommended constant observation of real scenery to his pupils; but also like Cézanne, he was absorbed with problems not so much representational as abstract—with, in his own words, "that which is produced by an interaction of the empty and the solid," with erecting new structures in a new space, with an intellectual reordering of the physical world. He was *not* interested in descriptive color (his use of simple warm and cool tones is another link with Cézanne), or in characterizing individual trees or rocks, or in effects of weather, season, light or shade, excepting a few perfunctory indications. It is important to realize all this in approaching Wang's works or those of a great many other literati painters; to stand before them and continue to talk, in the accepted manner, about the Chinese artist's profound penetration of nature, is much like maintaining that Cézanne's primary aim was to reveal the inner essence of his apples.

Early Ch'ing Painting: The Individualists

16

THE practice of retiring from human society during difficult periods of history was relatively free, in China, from the stigma of ivory-tower escapism. Under certain circumstances, such as those prevailing at the outset of a dynasty, and especially if the new rulers were foreign, it was seen not as evasion of civic responsibility but as ideal ethical conduct. Further resistance was futile, collaboration distasteful, and disengagement the only remaining course. Numerous precedents could be cited from the past, the most recent being the actions of the early Yüan scholars. Now in the early Ch'ing period many educated men renounced their lives of worldly affairs, either through physical withdrawal from the urban centers into Buddhist or Taoist monasteries, or through a psychological withdrawal into a private world of eccentricity, where they were exempted from social and political responsibilities by the traditional Chinese tolerance of erratic behavior.

In the cases of those who decided to enter religious orders, then, the decision was frequently dictated by a mixture of factors, practical and temperamental, which had little to do with religion proper. Some who became Buddhist monks did not even trouble to take the tonsure. Nor were many of the "recluses" genuine misanthropes; the severing of their attachment to urbane society was often formal and short-lived, and most of them continued to play some part in the secular intellectual community. An exception was K'un-ts'an, or Shih-ch'i, who seems to have had little liking for his fellow men. The fact that he became a Buddhist monk before the fall of Ming suggests a stronger spiritual motivation in his case, along with, perhaps, a more urgent desire for solitude. His own inscription on one of his works, a picture of a monk perched in a tree peering distrustfully downward, states his feelings strongly: "The question is how to find peace in a world of suffering. You ask how I came hither; I cannot tell the reason. I am living high up in a tree and looking down. Here I can rest free from all trouble, like a bird in its nest. People call me a dangerous man, but I answer: 'You are like devils.'"

K'un-ts'an's landscape painting, while it betrays some influence of Tung Ch'i-ch'ang in details, seems to derive more directly from observation of nature than do the landscapes of the orthodox masters in this same period. Some of his pictures evidently represent the particular scenery of places where he lived. Beginning with the first rise

K'un-ts'an (c. 1610-1693): The Pao-en Temple. Dated 1664. Detail from a hanging scroll.
Ink and colors on paper. Collection of the late Kanichi Sumitomo, Oiso (Japan).

of landscape painting in the fourth and fifth centuries, and continuing with its great development in the tenth, periods of political stress and the accompanying movement of educated men away from the cities had tended to stimulate innovations in this art, as the painters came once more into intimate contact with nature. Later occurrences of the phenomenon are less clear cut, and it is in no event a simple cause-and-effect matter. While a return to commonplace reality in its subjects, leaving the idealized realms of the late Sung Academy, is one aspect of Yüan dynasty landscape painting, another is the attitude of detachment that the painters develop toward these subjects, in line with the new ideals of the literati school. The situation in the early Ch'ing is even more complicated. Wang Shih-min and others inherit from the Ming masters the tradition of art-based-on-art, of stock motives and standard compositions, or else, like Wang Yüan-ch'i, engage in intellectualized manipulations of form. The individualists, meanwhile, exhibit on the one hand the most violent departures from visual truthfulness, and on the other appear to have turned back to nature for a reconsideration of the old concept of landscape painting as the outcome of a direct encounter between the artist's mind and the exterior world.

The subject of K'un-ts'an's most famous composition is the Pao-en Temple, which overlooked the Yangtze River near Nanking. The artist was living there in 1664 when he painted the picture, and reveals in it the fondness he felt toward these old buildings and their setting. He seems not to have imposed his will so severely upon them; in his crumbly, dry-brush drawing, they take on the unplanned and slightly disorderly air of reality. Bluff and knolls are earthy, there are no fantastic forms, all is on a reasonable scale. Thick streams of vapor flow down the slope and curl about the temple, reddened, along with the rest of the scene, by the glow of a setting sun. Most remarkable of all is the coloristic treatment of the distant hills, in which K'un-ts'an abandoned all considerations of strong or distinctive brushwork to capture in wet, sketchy strokes a quick impression of fading light.

K'un-ts'an's style exemplifies the quality that the Chinese critics term "luxuriance" or "denseness." A perfect illustration of its opposite, "sparseness," is to be seen in the painting of another Buddhist monk, Hung-jen, whose handscroll *Rivers and Mountains Without End* was painted three years earlier, in 1661. Hung-jen was born in Anhui Province, slightly to the west of the main cultural centers of the Chiang-nan region, and was the foremost painter of an Anhui School that flourished in the early Ch'ing period. The critics, and the painter himself in some inscriptions, assure us that he followed Ni Tsan in his landscapes; but so little of the Ni Tsan manner remains in his mature style, and that so thoroughly transformed, that it is difficult to distinguish more than a similarity in taste. What he shares with the Yüan master is a cleanness and clarity, best exemplified in a few of his most striking compositions and in some passages of his handscrolls, such as that reproduced here. He draws his angular rock towers in overlapping faces with long, straggly lines, lays on dilute washes of ink and occasionally the palest of colors, adds a sparse growth of wispy trees and bushes, a few toylike houses and a pavilion on the shore. The resulting landscape is like a construction of thin wires and glass, fragile and without solid substance. Still, it imparts a mood of lonely quiet, and seems a cool, very sensitive abstraction of mountain scenery viewed through clear air. The real world, however radically he may abbreviate and formalize it, lies just behind, unobscured by overlays of archaism or a preoccupation with brush techniques. In his odd way, then, Hung-jen represents another aspect of the return to nature.

Living in Nanking at the same time as K'un-ts'an, and perhaps acquainted with him, was another of the great individualists, Kung Hsien. He is credited as the leader of a Nanking School, but there was in fact no true school. He associated sometimes with a coterie of Nanking poets and scholars, composed of political dissidents who, like Kung himself, cherished nostalgic feelings for the fallen Ming regime. Most of the time, however, he kept to himself, living in a hut outside the city and cultivating his half-acre garden. A friend described him as "of an eccentric nature; only with difficulty does he get along with other people." He was singular also as a painter, and said of himself: "There has been no one before me, and will be no one after me." Kung Hsien professed some dependence on the past, as did virtually all Chinese painters—he speaks of having studied the works of Mi Yu-jen, for example, over a period of forty years—but he seems in the end to have chosen, like the other individualists, the lonely path into a new artistic province. The world of his paintings is wholly his own, existing only in terms of his private pictorial language.

This language is relatively simple, with a consistent syntax and a very limited vocabulary. The tireless reiteration of a few basic elements, strokes of similar size and shape, produces the larger forms, which in turn make up the composition. Dots of ink, clustered or scattered, purport to stand for ground vegetation, but serve primarily to give a special vibrancy to the surface. Countless short strokes are applied in overlay to define the shapes of rocks, or massed for tree foliage. The forms seem at times partially dissolved, existing as loose aggregations of particles. Where Hung-jen delineates and delimits sharply the objects in his landscapes, arranging them in orderly structures, Kung Hsien blurs their outlines and the distinctions between them, reducing the diversity of natural forms and phenomena to a strange homogeneity. Unusual also are the highlights and shadows on the rocks. The painter, who said of himself that his handling of ink was superior to his brushwork, subtly controls his scale of tone values from deepest black to the bare paper which he is fond of leaving in streaks about the composition, and so suggests a fitful play of light over the terrain. Dense white mists drift slowly along the ravines. Houses are seldom seen, and people never. This is a somber and forbidding vision, far removed from the Sung painters' "landscapes one can walk around in." No one is likely to feel any urge to enter Kung Hsien's paintings.

With the works of these three artists before us, there will scarcely be any need to point out that the refusal of the individualists to follow accepted modes and employ standard forms, their insistence on first-hand interpretations of reality, did not by any means lead to "realistic" styles. In a sense, their works still adhere to the literati concept of painting in being personal expressions; while they are products of an interaction between the artist's mind and the world outside it, the former remains the decisive

Hung-jen (c. 1603-1663): Rivers and Mountains without End. Dated 1661. Section of a handscroll.
Ink and light colors on paper. (H. 11¼″) Collection of the late Kanichi Sumitomo, Oiso (Japan).

Kung Hsien (c. 1620-1689): Trees in a Landscape. Section of a handscroll. Ink on paper. (H. 10⅜")
William Rockhill Nelson Gallery of Art, Kansas City.

factor. When the painter's temperament was odd, the paintings became very odd indeed. Yet Chinese painting never develops into a full-fledged non-objective art, however closely it may approach it, probably because, in the Chinese view, the expressive value of the pictures depended not only upon non-descriptive qualities of brushwork and form, but also on the ways in which the artist transformed visual appearances into the matter of art. Cut off altogether from its correlative in nature, the pictorial image would have lost most of its point. The same was true in calligraphy: the written character might be made quite illegible in the wilder modes of writing, but always stood in some relationship, however distant, to the standard script.

There is no better illustration of all this than the person and the painting of Chu Ta, who called himself Pa-ta Shan-jen. Born in 1625, he was a descendant of one branch of the Ming imperial family. Upon the fall of the dynasty, when he was about twenty, he became a Buddhist monk. Beyond that point his biography becomes obscure, since sources for it do not agree either on the events or on the order in which they occurred. He fell victim, it would appear, to a severe mental disturbance, which drove him continually into violent fits of elation and depression. At a certain moment in his life he affixed to his door a sign bearing the single character *ya*, "dumb"; and from that moment he never uttered a word to anyone. He laughed, cried, gesticulated, drank wine, wrote and painted, but never spoke. "When he felt inclined to write," recounts one of his contemporaries who composed a brief biography of him, "he would bare his arm and grasp the brush, at the same time emitting loud cries like a madman." Most of his paintings were done while he was drunk. The same biographer, writing without the benefit of modern psychology, expresses bewilderment that works of such power could be accomplished under these conditions. "Alas and alas," he exclaims, "one can get drunk as he did, but not crazy as he was!"

The accounts of Chu Ta's madness and drunkenness recall the life of Hsü Wei, and there are similarities also in their paintings, which suggest that some part of Chu's style was taken from the deranged Ming painter. But while Hsü's personal aberration manifested itself in an unleashed and passionate impulsion of the brush (p. 154), the characteristic works of Chu Ta convey rather a sense of constraint and repression that agrees with what we are told of the man himself. Painting was for Chu Ta a means of communication, and his use of it expressive but seldom truly fluent. His brush moves slowly, often with an odd twisting motion, which is to be observed especially when the stroke changes direction. Whatever impression of laxity and clumsiness it may give must be understood as purposeful deception; no brushline in Chinese painting is further from true weakness. Where the stroke was made with a brush unevenly loaded with ink, marked variations in tone appear within it. Spots of ink are sometimes applied so wet that the edges blur as the ink suffuses outward. At other points the stroke is dry and scratchy. Through all this variety of brushwork runs a constant and very distinctive quality, which prevents Pa-ta Shan-jen's works from being confused with those of any other painter—barring, of course, deliberate imitations. They seem tightly disciplined, but by inherent and mysterious rules that have little to do with ordinary canons of painting.

His pictures appear to be making particularized statements; one would be at a loss to translate them into verbal statements, but the artist himself was, after all, incapable of doing that. Are the misshapen birds that inhabit so many of his pictures, usually balancing unsteadily on one leg, symbols that had for the painter some definite meaning, or was this simply a private joke of which he never tired? Some of his birds and other creatures have square or lozenge-shaped eyes, the significance of which, if any, is equally unfathomable. He seems to endow them, at times, with human attributes: a crow, or a fish, will glower malevolently from the picture, and small fluffy birds such as those in our reproduction display more self-satisfaction than one would expect to encounter in the animal kingdom.

Chu Ta's landscapes carry the same bizarre taste into more intricate compositions. In the leaf from the landscape album in the Honolulu Academy of Arts, which is among his few works in color, a particular stroke, a bent arc, is repeated throughout the picture. This, with the insistent *tien*, horizontal and vertical—the former serving also as the foliage, and the latter as the trunks, of smaller trees—provides an extraordinary surface consistency. The whole structure is pulled forward to the picture plane by a scattering of dark accents and the contrived elimination of space. The painting agrees formally, then, with dominant tendencies in recent Occidental art. It preserves an additional dimension of meaning, however, by remaining a landscape, although a fantastic one, representing a tilted, boulder-strewn promontory on a river shore, dominated by a central spire.

The hanging scroll in the Shōkokuji, a Buddhist temple in Kyoto, is a landscape of a different sort, more sparse and less tightly knit in design, with even more of an air of improvisation. Evidences of change of plan are visible here and there, and ambiguous passages which are likely to have been only partially intentional. Despite a certain cold, withdrawn quality in them, Chu Ta's landscapes never appear so rationally controlled as, for example, those of Wang Yüan-ch'i. They are more subject to momentary, intuitive decisions, made by the artist as the painting proceeded. The twisting, rising progression of rocks and ridges cannot be understood logically at every point, nor is this a picture in which every stroke has a precise function and significance. Yet the landscape has the organic unity of a natural growth, and a monumentality that evokes echoes of the Northern Sung artists whom Chu Ta revered.

The supreme master among the individualists, the painter with greatest breadth of vision and the finest technician as well, was Tao-chi, also known as Shih-t'ao. Like Chu Ta, he was descended from one of the Ming emperors, and took the vows to become a Buddhist monk in 1644. He did not settle for long in any single place until his late years, which were mostly spent in and around the city of Yang-chou. Before that he traveled constantly, visiting friends and climbing the famous mountains in various parts of China. He followed the precepts of Kuo Hsi, absorbing sensory impressions from nature but trying also to "understand the hidden forces of heaven and earth." In setting forth his understanding in paintings, he depended very little on existing styles; he is perhaps the most inventive of all later artists. He states as a credo what was accepted, to varying degrees, by the other individualists as well: "When asked if I paint in the manner of the Southern or the Northern School, I reply with a hearty laugh that I do not know whether I am of a school, or the school of me; I paint in my own style."

Tao-chi's belief in the "single brushstroke" as "the origin of existence and root of the myriad phenomena," alluded to briefly at the beginning of this book, and his development of that theme in the first chapter of his treatise on landscape painting, establishes once more the mysterious affinity between natural and artistic creation which the Sung theorists had recognized. Once the artist has grasped this "method that is no-method," the principles with which all natural phenomena comply will govern also the formation of his paintings. Out of a diversity of visual stimuli he composes a limited and ordered system of forms which Victoria Contag, author of a study of Tao-chi and his treatise, has identified with the "second reality" of Confucian thought. By pondering his perceptions,

Chu Ta (1625-c. 1705): Two Birds. Album leaf. Ink on paper. (12½×10⅜″)
Collection of the late Kanichi Sumitomo, Oiso (Japan).

Chu Ta (1625-c. 1705): Landscape. Album leaf. Ink and light colors on silk. (9⅛×11″)
Honolulu Academy of Arts.

Chu Ta (1625-c. 1705): Landscape. Hanging scroll. Ink on paper. (62¼×18⅜″)
Shōkokuji, Kyoto.

▶

the artist becomes aware of the general in the particular, and a relationship between seemingly disparate parts. Tao-chi often portrayed the scenery of specific places, relying, no doubt, upon sketches or memories of his travels; but he so universalizes his experience that one mountain becomes all mountains.

Tao-chi (1641 - c. 1717): A Man in a House beneath a Cliff. Album leaf.
Ink and light color on paper. (9½×11″) Nü Wa Chai Collection.

The leaf in the superb album of the Nü Wa Chai collection represents a man in a hut built beneath an overhanging cliff. But the movement of line in the drawing of rocks is too grand, too sweeping, to be limited to particular objects, and the use of multiple contours suggests the artist's refusal to fix such limits. Tao-chi is not so much depicting rocks as presenting to our senses the forces that mold and destroy rocks. Experiencing empathically the movements of his hand as it wielded the brush, we take part in an awesome act of creation. As in the landscape album leaf by Chu Ta, a combination of calligraphic line and *tien* (Tao-chi introduces the novel method of applying them in colors, here light blue and brown) pulls the picture forward for the most immediate impact upon the viewer, besides supplying an extraordinary surface excitement. Tao-chi's leaf has even more of organic character than Chu Ta's; the lines that serve as contours and crevices of the rocks penetrate the forms as a vivifying network, like veins and arteries in a living thing.

His short handscroll illustrating T'ao Ch'ien's "Peach-blossom Spring" story achieves nearly the same intensity of pictorial excitement, diluted only slightly by the addition of literary content. It illustrates the tale of a fisherman who, by following a stream to its source among blossoming peach trees, discovered a hidden valley in which the descendants of refugees from the tyranny of the first Ch'in emperor had been dwelling in secluded peace for centuries. When he returned to his home and reported the existence

Tao-chi (1641-c. 1717): The Peach-Blossom Spring. Section of a handscroll.
Ink and colors on paper. (H. 9⅞″) Freer Gallery of Art, Washington, D.C.

of this Elysium, a search party was sent out to locate it; but the valley could never be found again. In Tao-chi's painting we see the fishing boat moored at the head of the stream, and the fisherman himself, still carrying his oar, being welcomed by the village elder. Powerfully-formed spurs of earth and rock, washed with deep green and spotted with colored *tien*, compartmentalize the composition, and divide the ideal, visionary realm from the mundane one. Houses, figures and trees are depicted with a childlike simplicity. Notably absent from the drawing are stereotyped forms and brushstrokes of a predetermined, "ready-made" character. Tao-chi, the advocate of "the method that is no-method," adapts his technique to his needs, often avoiding even a complete consistency within a single work. In spite of having thus sacrificed a fundamental unifying device, however, he succeeds in preserving in his pictures the indispensable quality of coherence.

A height of grandeur and universality is reached in Tao-chi's masterwork, the great *Waterfall on Mt. Lu*, a huge landscape painted on silk. The artist's inscription refers to Kuo Hsi, and appropriately: Tao-chi has indeed recaptured, for a brief moment, the precarious balance between subjective and objective modes of vision, which had been the triumph of Northern Sung landscape six centuries earlier. The painting is surely not an accurate rendition of a particular scene. Yet it could not have been achieved before the artist had acquired, through accumulated apprehensions of reality, a penetrating knowledge of light, mist, the nature and structure of mountains. Perhaps it is Tao-chi himself, the tireless climber of mountains, who stands on a jutting ledge near the bottom, attended by a patient friend. An image of quiescence, he gazes not up toward the waterfall, but down into the dense vapor that flows past, enveloping all but the top fringes of pine trees and lapping around his feet. Beyond is a misty hollow, which opens back into another; still another hollow lies further back, above an obscuring layer of fog, and another beyond that. The waterfall pours over sheer precipices, from one level of the vast chasm to the next. Mass and space seem to fuse, with the mists as flux. In the mind of the musing scholar, one feels, the worlds of matter and spirit are similarly reconciled by this overpowering vision.

In such works as these, the individualists of the early Ch'ing dynasty brought landscape painting to still another great culmination. They drew the materials of their paintings more directly from nature than had many of their scholar-artist predecessors and contemporaries, even though the worlds they created out of sensory data, through personal modes of organizing and generalizing, were sometimes so thoroughly transformed as to preserve only the most tenuous ties with the physical world. Their brush techniques were unorthodox and distinctive, but, except in the case of Chu Ta, seldom took on such an independently expressive function as they had in the works of some other literati painters. Their interpretations of reality were as individual as their pictorial styles, and,

Tao-chi (1641-c. 1717): The Waterfall on Mount Lu. Hanging scroll (upper section, with inscription, not included). ▶
Ink and light colors on silk. (w. 24½") Collection of the late Kanichi Sumitomo, Oiso (Japan).

like those of the Sung landscapists, depend ultimately on no extraneous philosophical or religious systems. The question of whether the artist was Buddhist, as was K'un-ts'an, or Confucianist, as Kung Hsien probably was, or one of the complex and personal mixtures exemplified by Chu Ta and Tao-chi, seems to have had little to do with the nature of the paintings. The landscapes stand as metaphysical statements in themselves, self-sufficient and compelling.

17

SOME time in the late seventeenth or early eighteenth century, Wang Yüan-ch'i wrote: "In painting of the late Ming period, there were mannerist tendencies and degenerate movements, of which the Che School was the worst of all... The corrupt practices of the Yang-chou and Nanking painters today are quite as bad as were those of the Che School, and anyone who aims at a mastery of brush and ink must take pains to avoid them."

It was the protest of a guardian of tradition—Wang, for all his originality, was that—against the growing favor with which stylistic unorthodoxy was being received. Kung Hsien in Nanking, Tao-chi in Yang-chou, and the other individualists treated in the previous chapter, while they had not founded true schools, had set persuasive examples; their admirers adopted less of their styles than of their attitude of refusal to be bound by conventions. Wang Yüan-ch'i and the other orthodox masters had their following as well, but it consisted of more or less slavish imitators of manners of painting already dangerously tinged with imitativeness, and came to nothing. Wang Yüan-ch'i's warning was heeded by few, and the strongest current in the eighteenth century was individualism. Its character was affected, however, by the fact that individualism now was not merely tolerated, but had become positively popular. The boldness of some eighteenth century eccentrics is the boldness of circus performers subduing well-tamed lions.

An example of how the new situation affected painting may be seen in the career of Kao Ch'i-p'ei, a Manchu by birth and an accomplished painter from the time he was eight years old. His landscapes in a conservative style were much admired at the imperial court, where he served in a high official post. Besides working in the traditional manner with a brush, however, he developed an elaborate technique of finger painting, not only employing the balls of his fingers and the side of his hand to apply broad streaks and washes of ink and color, but also growing one fingernail to extra length and splitting it like a pen, so that it could be used for drawing lines. The method was not entirely new, but still served to give an air of novelty to the pictures, and, along with Kao's virtuoso technique and lively imagination, to make them very much in demand. He eventually gave up the brush altogether, and his more meticulous style with it,

Kao Ch'i-p'ei (c. 1672-1734): Landscape with Tall Peaks. Album leaf.
Ink and light colors on paper. (10⅝×13″) Museum of Asiatic Art, Amsterdam.

to devote all his energies as an artist to the production of finger paintings. He is even said to have employed assistants to add the colors, so as to be able to increase his output.

It is not surprising, in view of this mass-production method, that the level of quality in his finger paintings is not uniformly high; too many of them seem more vigorous than refined, and some are unpleasantly coarse. Like many other artists in the late period, he is at his best in the album form, where he allows his imagination full freedom in sustaining variety among the motives and compositions of the successive leaves. The album of landscapes in the Museum of Asiatic Art, Amsterdam, is among the finest, containing a number of striking and original pages, of which we reproduce one. It presents a sinister vista of needle peaks and sickly trees, seen through the smoky atmosphere of sunset. At the foot of the tallest peak, in what should perhaps be understood as a valley, is a single house, forlorn-looking in this scarcely habitable place. The effects of the finger painting technique are evident in the scratchy line—a fingernail, however skillfully used, cannot produce so firm and continuous a line as a brush can— and in the overlaid streaks of wash. Chinese critics liken Kao's style to that of Wu Wei, and although it is figure painting they refer to, some resemblance can be seen also between the landscapes of the two (cf. p. 119): both combine rough, imprecise lineament with uneven washes of ink into which light color is blended freely. Some influence of the Che School lingers in the works of Kao Ch'i-p'ei, as Chinese writers remark.

Kao Feng-han (1683-after 1747): Peonies and Rocks. Dated 1734. Album leaf.
Ink and light colors on paper. (11¼×16¾") Osaka Municipal Museum (former Abe Collection).

With unorthodoxy now so generally accepted, independently inclined artists had little fear—or hope—of shocking their contemporaries. Kao Ch'i-p'ei, as a part-time, somewhat commercialized eccentric, appears in many of his works to have been trying his best to startle and impress, even at the risk of falling into what the Chinese term "vulgarity". Nevertheless, his brushwork (or, properly, fingerwork), for all its abandon, carries relatively little of true expressionist fervor. A more credible eccentric, but another whose wildness often seems forced, was Kao Feng-han. Like Kao Ch'i-p'ei, he appears in some of his works as a stylistic conservative, but is best known for pictures in a freer, more extemporaneous manner, especially those done after he had lost the use of his right arm through severe rheumatism and had begun to write and paint with his left. He is seen at his best in the album in the former Abe Collection, Osaka, from which we reproduce the first leaf. It is a swirling composition of swift, fluid line and clean washes of ink and cool colors. The outlines of the peony petals are repeated in the contours of the rocks, and the stamens of the flower in scattered patches of moss. Kao Feng-han gives some suggestion of volume to his rocks with graded wash, then negates it deliberately by writing a long inscription on the face of one of them. The whole seems in the end more a display of calligraphy than a proper picture, but as such it is a brilliant performance.

Kao Feng-han is sometimes connected loosely to the Yang-chou school, and has occasionally even been numbered among the Eight Eccentrics of Yang-chou, even though he was neither a native nor a resident of that city. The group known as the Eight Eccentrics properly includes three who can be recognized as major painters: Chin Nung, Hua Yen and Lo P'ing, and five of lesser rank, all of whom lived in Yang-chou for some portion of their lives. They gathered in the salons of rich merchants who had made their fortunes in the salt trade or some other variety of commerce, and who now competed as patrons of the arts, providing lavish entertainment for scholars, poets and painters. The special tone of Yang-chou culture in this period was set by such gatherings, at which wealth paid tribute to genius, and after genius, to eccentricity.

The most prominent among the Yang-chou painters around the middle of the eighteenth century was Chin Nung. Far from displaying any artistic talent at an early age, he began painting, we are told, only after turning fifty. In Chin Nung we may observe once more, in a compound that no scientific analysis will ever resolve, the ingredients of a genuine amateurish lack of proficiency and deliberate *gaucherie*. Su Tung-p'o had written that in literature "it is not skill that is hard to achieve, but awkwardness"; the same paradoxical notion had been applied to painting theory in the literati school, and a late Ming writer had gone so far as to advise against the cultivation of skill, on the grounds that innate awkwardness, once lost, could never be recaptured. Chin Nung guarded his amateurism carefully, allowing no technical refinements to spoil it. He was nonetheless proud of his paintings, and his admiration for them was shared by his contemporaries.

The leaf we have chosen from the album owned by Mr. H. C. Weng, which bears a poem in Chin's peculiar square-cut calligraphy, returns to the old theme of man enjoying nature. A youth gazes across a lotus pond from a covered walk, resting one foot on a low stool and leaning on the railing. The figure strikes an ungainly pose, but without revealing in it any very distinct quality of temperament or mood, aside from a simple relaxation. Similarly, the oddness of the composition seems not to result so much from expressionist distortion as from sheer disregard for conventional canons of arrangement. As in his other works, Chin Nung flattens his forms and composes them on the surface in conformity with a special system of proportions—needless to say, his own. His distinctive brushline is best seen here in the drawing of the figure and in the wavering lines of the architecture. Any suspicion that this unsteadiness in the drawing might be attributable merely to the effects of old age is dispelled by the firmly written inscription above. Throughout the picture, and most of all in the lush and colorful setting—the willow and other trees, the grassy shore, the pond itself—Chin Nung gives the impression of being as aimless and relaxed as his subject, and of having nothing more substantial to convey than the warm atmosphere of a summer day. The picture makes this genial statement with such untroubled assurance that one accepts it as somehow significant.

The most versatile and technically accomplished of the Yang-chou masters was Hua Yen. His pictures of birds, flowers and animals were highly praised in his time; his landscapes received less attention. One of his contemporaries criticized them for "leaving out too much." Today the best of his landscapes, especially those in album-leaf form, can be admired as small masterpieces of abbreviation. They recapture something of the lyricism of Southern Sung album leaves, although they are very different in style and reflect a less serious approach both to nature and to the art of painting, treating familiar themes with a light, sometimes playful touch. It is just this lightness, this hint that the painter himself did not take an entirely serious view of his subject, that saves from sentimentality such a picture as the one reproduced here, an evocation of autumnal feeling refined to a point just short of preciousness. A strolling scholar pauses to look pensively across the water at a distant peak, his attitude of passive contemplation implicit in his stance. A few red leaves drift down from the branches of the tallest tree, delicately enhancing the mild melancholy of the scene. Neither the dry-brush lineament, soft but never weak, nor the subtly off-balance composition carries any strong sense of purposeful non-conformism. The intensely conceived and sometimes somber visions of the seventeenth century individualists have given way to less ambitious creations in a warmer, gentler spirit. The artist seems no longer driven by any urge to set forth his private understanding of the world at large, or to remake it according to some grand design as a manifestation of his personal temperament, but is satisfied to muse quietly, a bit distantly, on small aspects of nature and human experience.

By the beginning of the last quarter of the century, all but one of the Eight Eccentrics were dead. Lo P'ing remained, a solitary survivor of the last major school in Chinese painting. His association with Chin Nung, who had been his teacher, had continued only about seven years before it was terminated by Chin's death. It is difficult to imagine what Lo, a painter of some facility, could have learned about painting technique proper from the determinedly amateurish Chin. One can suppose that he absorbed rather the

荷花開了
銀塘悄
新涼早碧
翅蜻蜓多
少大比
通身衣微
風曾那人
同裏纖手剝
蓮逢記

Chin Nung (1687-after 1764): A Youth Gazing across a Lotus Pond. Album leaf. Ink and colors on paper. (11×9½″)
H. C. Weng Collection, Scarsdale, New York.

江風三里五里明月前灣後灣
瑟瑟霜嚴到枕湘天庭染秋山

Hua Yen (1682-1765): An Autumn Scene. Dated 1729. Album leaf. Ink and light color on paper. (9×6⅜″)
Freer Gallery of Art, Washington, D.C.

special taste, along with some points of style, that had gained Chin his high esteem. Lo P'ing himself became one of Yang-chou's most popular painters, partly because he was regarded as Chin Nung's artistic heir, and partly also through a curious caprice of his own: he painted ghosts, and claimed that his pictures of them were based on first-hand observation. But this was another conscious eccentricity; the days when a painter could see ghosts, or detect spiritual essences in rocks and trees, were long past, and it was now difficult to transcend the matter-of-fact with any real conviction.

In the winter of 1798, less than a year before his death, Lo P'ing re-encountered briefly an old friend called I-an, whom he had not seen for nine years, and painted for him as a farewell present the picture with which we shall conclude our consideration of Chinese painting. It is simultaneously a portrait of his friend and of the T'ang poet Meng Hao-jan, whose fondness for blossoming plum is recalled in the branch held by the figure. Lo P'ing's poetic inscription refers to another poem, by Meng Hao-jan's great contemporary Li Po, in which Li tells of finding a line of poetry while wandering in the forest, and resolves to save it to present to his friend Meng, implying that Meng, of all people in the world, was the one who would best understand it and use it. Lo P'ing's allusion thus suggests, by analogy, the depth of his friendship with I-an. The old man stands beside a fantastically hollowed rock, his head slightly bent, inhaling the fragrance of the blossoms with conscious aestheticism. The sensitively drawn face wears a look of world-weary melancholy so intense as to seem a bit grotesque. But this is not caricature, or satire; it is the same subtle playfulness that gave its special flavor to the autumn scene of Hua Yen. It is a kind of undirected irony, serving only to suggest that emotions once presented seriously, with an implicit demand that they be taken at face value, can no longer be so treated, however sincerely they may be felt in actuality. In spite of this, perhaps partly because of it, the pathos of the figure is strangely affecting. Lo P'ing draws in a style derived largely from that of Ch'en Hung-shou (cf. p. 157), who had himself formed his figure style through half-serious play upon an archaic manner. The whole expressive character of the picture and its inscription thus depends upon an elaborate dialogue between present and past, between an individual of the highest sensibility and a cultural heritage of which he was perhaps excessively aware.

The painting contains so many levels of meaning as to invite one to read still more into it. Admitting this, we may still wonder, as we look at it, whether Lo P'ing was not conscious of standing near the end of a long evolution, contemplating the past with the same mild sadness as the figure he portrays. The painting sums up the special virtues of the last phases of that evolution, but also exemplifies the paradoxes and contradictions that had penetrated to the very heart of Chinese painting: awkwardness sublimated into a kind of skill, individuality manifested in archaism, straightforward feeling set forth through oblique allusions, serious points disguised as pleasantries. Every further degree of concern with such interplay of opposites, every additional layer of stylistic reference, had separated the artist that much more from the once-possible forthright approach to the world. Thirteen centuries had passed since Tsung Ping had gazed at the landscapes painted on the walls of his room and relived the travels of his youth, eight since Chao

Lo P'ing (1733-1799): Portrait of the Artist's Friend I-an. Dated 1798. Section of a hanging scroll
(cropped at top and bottom). Ink and light colors on paper. (w. 17¼″) Private Collection, Washington, D.C.

Ch'ang had held a flower in his hand and "transcribed it" in painting. A good part of the later history of Chinese painting testifies that withdrawal from nature as a direct source for the content of an art need not mean the death of that art; but when the withdrawal has proceeded so far as this, when simple aesthetic values have been so thoroughly replaced by those so very sophisticated, the sustaining of a high level of quality requires artists more sensitive, and endowed with more creative force, than were to appear after Lo P'ing. The rest of Chinese painting was to remain, although not always so explicitly as Lo P'ing's work and seldom so movingly, a meditation upon the past.

Table of Dynasties

Selected Bibliography · Index of Names

List of Colorplates

Table of Dynasties

Han	206 B.C. - 221 A.D.
Chin, Three Kingdoms and Six Dynasties Periods	221 - 589
Sui	589 - 618
T'ang	618 - 906
Five Dynasties	906 - 960
Sung	960 - 1279
Northern Sung	960 - 1127
Southern Sung	1127 - 1279
Yüan	1279 - 1368
Ming	1368 - 1644
Ch'ing	1644 - 1911

Selected Bibliography

of Books and Articles on Chinese Painting in Western Languages

General

JAMES F. CAHILL, *Chinese Painting, 11th-14th centuries*, Crown Publishers, New York 1960.

VICTORIA CONTAG, *The unique characteristics of Chinese landscape pictures*, in Archives of the Chinese Art Society of America, v. VI, 1952, p. 45-63.

JEAN-PIERRE DUBOSC, *A new approach to Chinese Painting*, in Oriental Art, n.s., v. III, 1950, p. 50-57.

SHERMAN E. LEE, *Chinese Landscape Painting*, The Cleveland Museum of Art, Cleveland 1954. (New edition in preparation.)

ALAN PRIEST, *Aspects of Chinese Painting*, Macmillan, New York 1954.

SHŪJIRŌ SHIMADA and YONEZAWA YOSHIHO, *Painting of Sung and Yüan Dynasties*, Mayuyama Ryūsendō, Tokyo 1952.

LAURENCE SICKMAN and ALEXANDER SOPER, *The Art and Architecture of China*, Penguin Books, London and Baltimore 1956.

OSVALD SIRÉN, *Chinese Painting, Leading Masters and Principles*, Lund Humphries, London 1956-1958.

PETER C. SWANN, *Chinese Painting*, Editions Pierre Tisné, Paris 1958. (English and French editions.)

ARTHUR WALEY, *An Introduction to the Study of Chinese Painting*, Charles Scribner's Son, New York 1923.

YONEZAWA YOSHIHO, *Painting in the Ming Dynasty*, Mayuyama Ryūsendō, Tokyo 1956.

Individual Artists and Special Subjects

BIJUTSU KENKYŪSHO, Tokyo, *Liang K'ai*, Benridō, Kyoto 1957. (Japanese text with English résumé)

JAMES F. CAHILL, *Ch'ien Hsüan and his figure paintings*, in Archives of the Chinese Art Society of America, v. XII, 1958, p. 11-29.

JAMES F. CAHILL, *Confucian elements in the theory of painting*, in Arthur Wright, ed., *The Confucian Persuasion*, Stanford University Press, Stanford, Calif., 1960.

HELEN BURWELL CHAPIN, *A long roll of Buddhist images in the Palace Museum*, in Journal of the Indian Society of Oriental Art, v. IV, 1936, p. 1-24, 116-125; v. VI, 1938, p. 26-67. (Concerns the handscroll painted by Chang Sheng-wen.)

VICTORIA CONTAG, *Die beiden Steine*, Hermann Klemm, Brunswick c. 1950. (Concerns the painters K'un-ts'an and Tao-chi.)

VICTORIA CONTAG, *Die sechs berühmten Maler der Ch'ing Dynastie*, E.A. Seeman, Leipzig c. 1940. (Concerns the Four Wangs, Yün Shou-p'ing and Wu Li.)

RICHARD EDWARDS, *The landscape art of Li T'ang*, in Archives of the Chinese Art Society of America, v. XII, 1958, p. 48-60.

RICHARD EDWARDS and TSENG HSIEN-CHI, *Shen Chou at the Boston Museum*, in Archives of the Chinese Art Society of America, v. VIII, 1954, p. 31-46.

WEN FONG, *A letter from Shih-t'ao to Pa-ta-shan-jen and the problem of Shih-t'ao's chronology*, in Archives of the Chinese Art Society of America, v. XIII, 1959, pp. 22-53.

JAN FONTEIN, *Een album van Kao Ch'i-p'ei*, Bulletin of the Rijksmuseum, Amsterdam 1956, No. 3, p. 67-71.

HERBERT FRANKE, *Dschau Mong-fu, das Leben eines chinesischen Staatsmannes, Gelehrten und Künstlers unter der Mongolenherrschaft*, in Sinica, v. XV, 1940, p. 25-48.

HERBERT FRANKE, *Zur Biographie des Pa-ta shan-jen*, in *Asiatica, Festschrift Friedrich Weller*, Otto Harrassowitz, Leipzig 1954, p. 119-130.

ASCHWIN LIPPE, *Kung Hsien and the Nanking School*, in Oriental Art, n.s. v. II, 1956, p. 21-29; v. IV, p. 159-170.

MAX LOEHR, *A landscape attributed to Wen Cheng-ming*, in Artibus Asiae, v. XXII, no. 1/2, 1959, p. 143-152.

BENJAMIN ROWLAND, *The problem of Hui-tsung*, in Archives of the Chinese Art Society of America, v. V, 1941, p. 5-22.

SHŪJIRŌ SHIMADA, *Concerning the "i-p'in" style of painting* (transl. by James Cahill), in Oriental Art (to be published in near future).

OSVALD SIRÉN, *Shih-t'ao, painter, poet and theoretician*, in Östasiatiska Samlingarna, Bulletin n° 21, Stockholm 1949, p. 31-62.

ALEXANDER SOPER, *Early Chinese landscape painting*, in The Art Bulletin, v. XXIII, 1941, p. 141-164.

ALEXANDER SOPER, *Life-motion and the sense of space in early Chinese representational art*, in The Art Bulletin, v. XXX, 1948, p. 167-186.

WERNER SPEISER, *T'ang Yin*, in Ostasiatische Zeitschrift, 11. Jahrg., Heft 1/2, 1935, p. 1-21; Heft 3/4, p. 96-117.

Sir AUREL STEIN, *The Thousand Buddhas*, B. Quaritch, Ltd., London 1921. (Concerns the paintings found at Tun-huang.)

Michael Sullivan, *On the origin of landscape representation in Chinese art*, in Archives of the Chinese Art Society
of America, v. VII, 1953, p. 54-65.

Michael Sullivan, *Pictorial art and the attitude toward
nature in ancient China*, in The Art Bulletin, March 1954,
p. 1-19.

Tseng Yu-ho, *Notes on T'ang Yin*, in Oriental Art,
n.s. v. II, 1956, p. 103-108.

Tseng Yu-ho, *A report on Ch'en Hung-shou*, in Archives
of the Chinese Art Society of America, v. XIII, 1959,
pp. 75-88.

Tseng Yu-ho, *The "seven junipers" of Wen Cheng-ming*,
in Archives of the Chinese Art Society of America, v. VIII,
1954, p. 22-30.

Arthur Waley, *A Catalogue of Paintings Recovered
from Tun-huang by Sir Aurel Stein*, The British Museum,
London 1931.

Archibald Gibson Wenley, *"Clearing autumn skies over
mountains and valleys" attributed to Kuo Hsi*, in Archives
of the Chinese Art Society of America, v. X, 1956, p. 30-41.

Nelson Wu, *The toleration of eccentrics*, in Art News,
May, 1957, pp. 27-29, 52-54. (Concerns the early Ch'ing
individualist painters.)

Index of Names and Subjects

List of Colorplates

PUBLISHED MARCH 1985

PRINTED BY
IMPRIMERIES RÉUNIES SA
LAUSANNE

PHOTOGRAPHS

All the works reproduced in this volume, including those in Formosa and Japan, were photographed by Henry B. Beville, Washington, except the following: pages 10, 14 (photographs by Zoltan Wegner, London), pages 13, 21, 128 (photographs by the Sandak Company, Boston), pages 73, 152, 157, 186, 190 (photographs by Paul I. Bessem, Amsterdam), page 166 (photograph by Hans Hinz, Basel).

PRINTED IN SWITZERLAND